A PARENT'S GUIDE TO
TEENAGE SEXUALITY

A PARENT'S GUIDE TO TEENAGE SEXUALITY

Jay Gale, Ph.D.

An Owl Book

Henry Holt and Company

New York

Copyright © 1989 by Jay Gale, Ph.D.
All rights reserved, including the right to reproduce
this book or portions thereof in any form.
Published by Henry Holt and Company, Inc.,
115 West 18th Street, New York, New York 10011.
Published in Canada by Fitzhenry & Whiteside Limited,
195 Allstate Parkway, Markham, Ontario L3R 4T8.

Library of Congress Cataloging-in-Publication Data
Gale, Jay.
A parent's guide to teenage sexuality / Jay Gale. — 1st ed.
p.   cm.
Bibliography: p.   Includes index.
ISBN 0-8050-0937-X
ISBN 0-8050-1648-1 (An Owl Book: pbk.)
1. Sex instruction — United States 2. Teenagers — United States —
Sexual behavior. 3. Parenting — United States. 4. Hygiene,
Sexual — Study and teaching (Secondary) — United States. I. Title.
HQ57.G35   1989
306.7'088055 — dc19   88-39428
                                                            CIP

Henry Holt books are available at special discounts for bulk
purchases for sales promotions, premiums, fund-raising,
or educational use. Special editions or book excerpts can
also be created to specification. For details contact:
Special Sales Director, Henry Holt and Company, Inc.,
115 West 18th Street, New York, New York 10011.

First Owl Book Edition — 1991

Illustrations by Scott E. Carroll
Printed in the United States of America
Recognizing the importance of preserving the written word,
Henry Holt and Company, Inc., by policy, prints all of its
first editions on acid-free paper. ∞
1   3   5   7   9   10   8   6   4   2

Grateful acknowledgment is made to the following for permission to
reprint excerpts from their publications: Little, Brown and Company,
Male Sexuality, by Bernie Zilbergeld, Ph.D., copyright © 1978 by
Bernie Zilbergeld; Bantam, Doubleday, Dell, *Fatherhood*, by Bill
Cosby, copyright © 1986 by William H. Cosby, Jr.; Simon and Schuster,
Raising a Child Conservatively in a Sexually Permissive World, by Sol
Gordon, Ph.D., and Judith Gordon, copyright © 1983, 1989 by Sol and
Judith Gordon; Macmillan Publishing Company, Inc., *Teenage Sexuality*,
by Aaron Hass, Ph.D., copyright © 1981 by Aaron Hass; Raymond
Lovett, Ph.D., for "An Expert Tries to Explain to His Son the
Facts of, er, Life," © 1984 Raymond Lovett, which appeared
in the *Los Angeles Times*, Sept. 4, 1984.

CONTENTS

List of Illustrations   ix

Introduction   xi

I.   YOUR ROLE IN YOUR CHILD'S SEX EDUCATION

1. Your Child Will Receive a Sex Education, Whether   3
   You Like It or Not
2. Finding a Beginning Point   13
3. Understanding the Obstacles   21
4. Methods of Sex Education   28
5. The Rodney Dangerfield Factor: Everybody Needs   35
   Respect
6. A Quick Primer on Communicating with   43
   Your Teenager

II.   WHAT YOUR TEENAGER NEEDS TO KNOW

7. Your Teenager Needs More Than Facts   55
8. Preparation for Puberty   61
9. Touching and Sexual Intimacy   67
10. Conception and Contraception   74

Contents

11. The Truth about AIDS   95
12. Sexually Transmitted Diseases   102
13. Homosexuality: The Fears and the Realities   110
14. Preventing Sexual Exploitation   118

III. SPECIAL SITUATIONS, SPECIAL NEEDS

15. The Sexually Active Teenager   133
16. Pregnancy   140
17. Dealing with Sexual Trauma   151
18. If You're a Single Parent   159
19. The Homosexual Teenager   167
20. The Handicapped Teenager   176

    Afterword   191
    Appendix: Finding Help   193
    Glossary   203
    Notes   219
    Bibliography   225
    Index   233

ILLUSTRATIONS

1. The Uterus and Fertilization   75
2. How to Use a Condom   84
3. How to Use Contraceptive Foam   86
4. How to Use a Diaphragm   90
5. How to Use a Contraceptive Sponge   93

INTRODUCTION

Whenever I read a "how-to" book about teenagers or children, I always feel a little intimidated and stupid. I guess my first reaction is, "Do good parents really do that? I don't know if I can!" Sometimes I wonder about the author: "Does he really follow his own advice?" "I bet he's a perfect parent"—or just the opposite: "Boy, I bet he really screwed up his kids." Sometimes I wonder whether the author even has any kids.

As an introduction to this book, let me answer some of these questions for you. I think the advice I am giving is good, sound advice. I wouldn't have written this book if I didn't think I had something to offer. No, I didn't follow every bit of my own advice as my two children progressed through their adolescence. Some of what I will tell you I learned later, when it was no longer appropriate to my children, and some of it I didn't realize was all that important until after the right time had passed.

I believe that my son and my daughter have survived their adolescence intact, and that they, myself, and my wife are better people and a closer family for all we have gone through. Yes, both our teenagers rebelled in their own ways; yes, we went through our share of family counseling; yes, there were times when we felt we couldn't cope; yes, there were times when the tension affected our marriage; and no, neither of us are perfect or even near-perfect parents. Yes, there were times when we lost our cool and weren't sure who was crazier, us or the kids; and yes, both our children are independent, achieving, good people with their own idiosyncrasies and imperfections.

Neither of my children had as perfect a sex education as I describe in this book, but both were prepared more than adequately.

The bottom line is that I am not a perfect parent, and neither are you. I didn't follow all of my own advice, and neither will you. However, if you read this book thoroughly, there is a great deal that no doubt will make sense to you. Use what you feel fits your personality and your ability as a person. Don't castigate yourself for what you do not do. I am doing the best job I am capable of doing as a parent, and just the fact that you are reading this book tells me that you are doing the best job that you can; not perfect, but the best you are capable of under your circumstances.

As a therapist, I find that the two most important ingredients leading to positive changes in an individual, a marriage, or a family are the motivation of the clients and the skills that they learn. Raising children successfully takes a great deal of motivation and skill. So does providing your teenager with an adequate sex education. The fact that you have chosen to read a book to help you educate your teenager about sex is an indication that you have the motivation. This book can provide you with many of the necessary skills.

Please note that throughout this book teenagers are usually referred to in the masculine (he, his, him, etc.) rather than in phrases like "he or she." This is not meant to be sexist in any way, nor is it meant to indicate that this book does not apply equally to young women. I've chosen this style simply to keep sentences from being too awkward and to make reading less complicated.

I

YOUR ROLE IN YOUR CHILD'S SEX EDUCATION

1

YOUR CHILD WILL RECEIVE A SEX EDUCATION, WHETHER YOU LIKE IT OR NOT

Whether you like it or not, your child is getting a sex education. You don't have a choice *whether* he gets an education; your only choice is *how* it takes place. Every day, your child is being bombarded by information about sex: from his friends, from movies or TV programs, from newspapers, novels, *Playboy*-type magazines, and even from the lyrics in many current songs. It may take the form of a friend bragging about exaggerated exploits or of a movie or video in which a woman is easily seduced by the machismo of her lover, but all of it gets absorbed on some level. It may be information gleaned from a newspaper article about AIDS or propaganda contained in an advertisement for feminine hygiene spray, but again, it is part of his sex education. Some of the information will be fact, and some will be fiction. But unless your child has some reliable sources, he will be incapable of distinguishing one from the other.

Probably the greatest source of information about sex and sexuality for teenagers is their parents. Every time your adolescent hears you comment about a pregnant relative or whisper about a neighbor's abortion, he learns a little more. Even if you never say a word about sex, you are still educating him. Your silence may convey a feeling of embarrassment and reluctance to talk about sex or possibly a lack of concern or even disapproval. However, in one way or another it does convey a message. *You are communicating, and your child is getting a sex education!*

If you do talk openly with your child about sex, the question becomes, is he getting all the necessary information? Sex is a very complicated subject involving biological, moral, emotional, social, and medical considerations. No parent, no matter how expert in the subject, is capable of discussing every one of these complex issues. And, even if you could, do you realistically think that your child is going to sit there for the hours it would take? Unless I put a refrigerator full of food in front of my kids, it's hard to get them to sit down for five consecutive minutes.

Besides, most children are reluctant to talk openly with their parents about sex. Their usual response goes something like "Oh, Mom, come on, I know everything I need to know," or is simply an embarrassed look and then an uncomfortable silence while you give your speech. Talking to adolescents about sex is not easy, either for the parent or for the teenager.

Yet it is essential that they get the necessary information. Adolescents do not put off being sexual just because they are uninformed. One fact is exceptionally clear: teens are definitely sexual people.

- According to the Alan Guttmacher Institute, a reproductive health research center, more than one million teenage girls get pregnant every year.
- In 1987 there were two hundred thousand *reported* cases of sexually transmitted diseases in young people under

4

the age of twenty; seven thousand of these were in children between the ages of ten and fourteen. (These are *reported* cases; most sexually transmitted diseases go unreported.)[1]
• Eighteen percent of girls who are teenagers today will have an abortion before their twentieth birthday.[2]

Facing Reality

The reality is that your teen is a sexual person and thinks about sex. The reality is that your teen is learning about sex every day and that you are doing part of the teaching. The reality is that you cannot control every fact (or myth) your child learns about sex, but you will in one way or another significantly affect his attitudes and his education about sex. Your choices are clear; you can provide him with dependable information to lessen the impact of the many inaccuracies he will be faced with, or you can allow him to sort out for himself what is truth and what is fiction. Adolescents *need* clear information about sex, presented to them at their own level and at a time when they are ready to digest it.

Your child will be faced with numerous decisions concerning his sexuality throughout his adolescence and for the rest of his life. There is no way you can protect him from making mistakes. However, the more accurate information your teen has about the complex issues of sexuality, and the more he has thought out his options, the fewer risks he faces. The goal of this book is to assist you in helping your child make the most informed decisions about sex that he is capable of making.

It used to be that the ultimate consequences of making an uninformed decision about sex were either catching a sexually transmitted disease or pregnancy; certainly both are very serious consequences. However, the hazard now is even more dramatic. *The risk to your child of not having all the facts is death.* There are projections that the next at-risk population for AIDS is teenagers. As of October 1988, more than forty-two thousand Americans were dead of this disease, and as many as three million are estimated to carry its deadly virus. A recent report indicated that as of May 1988 the number of AIDS cases among people thirteen to nineteen years old was nearly double the number from a year earlier, and more than triple the number diagnosed with the disease in May 1986.[3] *This is a dangerous time for your child to have inaccurate information about sex.*

This is not another "what you should be doing if you were a good parent" type of book. It is designed to help you decide what kind of a role you want to play in your teenager's sex education, and then to help you carry out that role to the fullest of your capabilities. If you want to be an active participant in his education, this book will teach you the skills to communicate directly. If you want to take a more passive role, it will give you the resources to tap, so that your child can get a complete sex education with a minimum of intervention on your part. Even if you are not yet certain what tack you want to take, or if you are just slightly uncomfortable with the thought of discussing sex openly with your teenager (as most parents are), this book will assist you in assessing how active you want your role to be.

The purpose of this book is to help you educate your child no matter what your beliefs are about morality and sexuality. I will neither preach to you nor challenge your values. Whether you are against premarital sex or accept it, whether you support a woman's right to have an abortion or oppose it, or whether you support or oppose such issues as gay rights or woman's liberation, this book can be helpful to you. Only one major value judgment is made, namely that it is better for teens to be accurately informed about sex than to be randomly misinformed by leaving their sex education to chance. Other than that, I will attempt to present information in a factual, nonjudgmental manner. This book aims to help you, the parent, determine what you want to communicate to your teenager and how best to transmit the information.

The Myth of the Sex Lecture

I remember the fantasy clearly. I'd sit my son down in a nice quiet setting, put my arm around him, and share with him all there is to know about the beauties of love, sex, and life in general. A warm, touching scene between father and son. I looked forward to this magic moment; but also I feared it. For years I worried about what I was going to say when the time came. Here I was an expert in the field of sexuality, and I didn't know what to say!

In my mind I vacillated between the thrill of victory and the agony of defeat; one day fantasizing about this incredible chance at intimacy with my child, and the next, worrying about how I was going to cram everything there is to know about sex into one brief lecture. This is The Myth of the Sex Lecture. The fantasy is a common one among parents— as is the fear that accompanies it.

It took me a long time, but I finally figured out that you cannot squeeze enough information into one lecture—or even a series of lectures—to adequately educate your child about sex. There is a tremendous amount of information that adolescents need to know if they are going to mature into well-adjusted adults. It's hard enough to know what to say to your adolescent about sex, but if you think you have only one shot at it, it's impossible. Sex education is an ongoing process, one that will encompass the rest of your child's life, just as it has your own entire life. All you can do is open the door for your child, walk him through the first few steps, and leave him with a sense of comfort so that he can take the rest of the journey with a feeling of ease and healthy interest.

Other Common Fears about Educating Your Child

The Myth of the Sex Lecture is not the only impediment that stands between parents and their teenagers when it comes to sex education. Even though you love your child and you rationally understand the need for a comprehensive sex education, you may find that you experience one or more of the common fears listed below.

The Fear of Stimulating Sexual Interest

Probably the most common fear among parents about sex education is that if they explain the facts of life or teach their kids about the intricacies of sexuality, it will somehow lead to increased sexual interest, sexual activity, and even promiscuity. This argument has been used successfully in many locales to keep sex education out of the public schools. However, the research clearly shows otherwise. A research program conducted by Johns Hopkins University to evaluate a school-based pregnancy prevention program for inner-city girls found not only a dramatic decrease in the number of pregnancies, *but also that girls who participated in the program postponed intercourse longer than girls who did not participate.*[4] Similarly, the Netherlands, which openly disseminates information about specific sexual matters on TV, radio, and in magazines, and Sweden, which has had a compulsory sex education program in its schools since 1956, have among the lowest teenage pregnancy rates in the world.[5] By contrast, the United States, with only two states (New Jersey and Maryland) and the District of Columbia mandating sex education in the schools, has the highest pregnancy rate in the world among developed nations.[6]

Clearly, it does not appear that sex education programs lead to promiscuity. On the contrary, the evidence shows that they result in lower pregnancy and abortion rates, delays in date of first intercourse, and in a greater sense of sexual responsibility.

The Fear of Not Knowing Enough

The fear of not knowing enough seems to derive from The Myth of the Sex Lecture discussed earlier. Many parents think that it is their duty to sit down and lecture their children about many aspects of sexuality that they do not feel informed enough about themselves. In fact few parents can adequately teach their children all the biological and medical intricacies of sex, not to mention the emotional and mechanical aspects. You are not an expert in the field. And even the experts may have difficulty educating their children about sex. Psychologist Raymond E. Lovett, Ph.D., writes about an encounter with his son[7]:

"Hey, Dad, do men have sex hormones?" my 11-year-old son piped from behind his sports magazine.

The question pierced my soul, tensed my muscles; within me adrenaline gates lifted, pouring paternal anxiety throughout

9

my body. Jerking to an erect sitting position, I dropped my spoon, which first rang loudly at the cereal bowl. As it hit the floor it shook, drumroll-like, anticipating my response. I had to answer, my son was waiting for an answer. From me. About hormones. About male hormones. The silence tensed my tongue. This is it. The time is now. I had prepared. This was the milestone. It was "the first sexual inquiry."

This is not how I planned it. I had hoped "it" would come while he and I were alone in the woods, in the spring, perhaps in a park, but at least outside, in nature, with reliable props like flowers and animals. I had hoped for a cow and, yes, selfishly for a bull, too.

Now, here I was at breakfast, unshaven, half awake, vulnerable to interruptions from the wife and a younger brother.

After giving his son a lengthy lecture on androgens, testosterone, eggs, seeds, hair growth, et cetera, the conversation continues.

"I just wanted to know if men had male hormones like this woman here." He pointed to a masculine-looking woman runner in his magazine. "The article talks about women with male hormones. I wondered if men have them, too. No big deal, Dad. See ya."

He was out the door, my mouth open, my sex ed speech frustrated, obsessions, like a firecracker string fused by fear, popped in my head.

I've ruined his sex life.

I gave him too much information. Not enough. The wrong kind. Erroneous.

. . . As I pick up the sports magazine with the linebacker-size female hurdler grimacing at me, a second magazine falls from the pages. There before me is last winter's swimsuit issue, open and folded to a flat crease to pages of bikini beauties. Relief. My son's hormones have redeemed my dull speech. I silently hope that he is giggling with his friends somewhere.

As a parent, the amount of your specific knowledge about sexuality is really not the issue. As you will see in chapter 4, you can successfully fulfill this important responsibility without any real expertise.

The Fear of Being Repetitive

When you give your child any sort of information about sex, or even hint at it, you are likely to hear such replies as "Leave me alone, I know all that stuff," or "We already learned all that in school." Don't let him fool you. What he knows about sex can probably fit into a thimble. He may know the basics of reproduction, and maybe a combination of truths and lies about such vital topics as sexually transmitted diseases, contraception, and the physiology of sex, but chances are that fact and fiction are so tightly interwoven that he doesn't have a realistic idea of how to take proper precautions against an unwanted pregnancy or a sexually transmitted disease. Even if your child has had a sex education class in school, it might have been geared simply to the biology of reproduction and might not have included sufficient information about being sexually responsible or about the emotional aspects of sexuality.

The Fear of Embarrassment

In a sense, this is a realistic fear. Most parents do feel somewhat embarrassed or uncomfortable in discussing the various aspects of sexuality with their teenagers. Likewise, most teenagers, although looking for information from their parents, feel equally awkward. However, there are a lot of things in our lives that are a little embarrassing or that cause us discomfort, but that we still do anyway. We do them because we know the consequences of not doing them. Take as an example undressing for the first time in the high school locker room. You would rather not do it, but if you don't you fail physical education.

Think for a second about the consequences of your child not understanding the realities of conception, contraception, and sexually transmitted diseases. Are you willing to risk a small degree of embarrassment to keep your child from an unwanted pregnancy or from ending up with AIDS or some other sexually transmitted disease? The risks of not practicing safe sex are enormous in our present environment.

The Fear that My Teenager Isn't Ready for the Information

Every parent has to judge when his or her teenager is ready for sex information. However, as parents we often have a tendency to deny how fast our children are growing. Do not continually kid yourself that your child is not ready. The following statistics taken from prominent surveys of teenagers are sobering. By age fifteen, 43 percent of girls reported that they had touched a boy's penis[8] and 55 percent of boys had touched a girl's vagina.[9] By age eighteen, 53 percent of girls and 46 percent of boys reported having had intercourse.[10]

The reality is that your teenager is a sexual person. Even if he is not sexually active at the present time, it probably won't be long before he is. It will not be your discussions about sex that will stir his interest in sex; it will be his biological clock. The topic of sex is awkward for just about all of us, but it is essential to talk to your teen if you are going to protect him from the dangers of indiscriminate sexuality while introducing him to its intimate potential.

2

FINDING A
BEGINNING POINT

It's easy for experts to talk about what you *should* do as a parent. After all, they don't live inside your home, with your child and your set of circumstances; nor do they suffer from the same anxieties and fears as you do. Sure there is a textbook way to handle situations, but, realistically, few of us are capable of approaching life that way. It's great to have ideals by which we wish to live, but it is equally important to accept our limitations as human beings and as parents.

This chapter has little to do with ideals. It is concerned with you and your child. Not Beaver Cleaver or some imaginary ideal, just you and your child. It is designed to help you determine a comfortable starting point to initiate your child's sex education. In addition, it lays the groundwork for later chapters that will explore what information to give to your teen and how you can most effectively present it.

Early Subliminal Sex Education

In a sense your child's sex education began the day he was born or possibly even before. The name you picked out for him, the color you painted his room, the toys you gave him, and the games you played all came with expectations attached. It's impossible not to have dreams for your children, and each of these dreams comes with an expectation. It is from these dreams, these expectations, and your actions toward your children that they begin to build their sense of "gender identity," their feeling of maleness or femaleness. Certainly there are many other factors that add to this early definition of sexual self; nonetheless, your role as a parent is a cornerstone of this earliest sex education.

Likewise, the ease and comfort with which you touch your child and allow him to touch you affects his sexual interactions in later life. If touching and holding are treated as natural and enjoyable parts of the parent-child interaction, caressing and being caressed will likely be more comfortable for the maturing adolescent during his early sexual experiences. On the other hand, if touching and holding are an uncomfortable part of the parent-child interaction, or if this physical contact is tainted by seductive or sexual overtones from the parent or other adults, your child's ability to be physically intimate as an adolescent or an adult will likely be adversely affected. In addition, the relationship that you and your partner model for the child will give him a standard against which to compare future relationships of his own. If your relationship is caring and loving, certainly it makes it more likely that your child will learn to be affectionate. If, on the other hand, your interactions with partners are cold or aloof, he may begin to view this as the norm in adult relationships.

Admittedly, this summary is not at all an exhaustive analysis of how children learn about sexuality from parents prior to any so-called formal sex education. These are not the only ways in which your child learns about sex from you, nor are they the only sources from which your child gets his subliminal sex education. There are many other major influences, such as television, movies, and peers, just to name a few. The point is that you were influencing your child's adult sexuality long before your child's sex education became even a thought in your mind.

Understanding Your Own Discomfort

One major obstacle that will probably get in your way when you are seeking a beginning point for your adolescent's sex education is your conflicting feelings toward your own sexuality. All of us are pulled in a variety of directions by complex thoughts, feelings, and fantasies. Your sexual values lead you in one direction, while possibly your ideals for your child's sexuality tug in another. The morals you were raised with are still an active influence on your sexual beliefs and activities. Yet they may be in conflict with your desire to be a progressive parent. A part of you is motivated to protect your child, but another part knows that he must be allowed to become independent. Even your level of satisfaction or dissatisfaction with your own sexuality becomes part of the final equation.

We are pulled in so many directions, yet with all of this inner dissonance, we expect ourselves to share a consistent, educational, life-directing message about sexuality with our children. It is from these disparities that our conflict arises. And it is the depth and the nature of these inner conflicts that affect our comfort level in discussing sex.

As the saying goes, however, there is some good news and some bad news about these inner struggles. The bad news is that virtually all of us experience this conflict to some degree. Even if you are perfectly content with your own sexuality, it is indeed a rare person that experiences total harmony in the face of all the conflicting messages we get from our environment.

Now for the good news! No matter how deep the conflict you feel, you are capable of providing your teenager with a sound sex education. The level of your comfort will determine not *whether* you are capable of educating your adolescent about sex, but rather *how* you approach this undertaking. Even if you know that the topic is terribly uncomfortable or painful for you to discuss, you are capable of providing him with the necessary tools.

How Do You Know Where to Start?

As a sex therapist, I speak to many people every year about the most intimate aspects of their sexuality, and I rarely encounter any hesitation on their part to discuss the matter openly. Yet when I first began my training in this field, my hesitation to ask questions, along with my blushing and obvious discomfort, made information gathering much more difficult both for me and for the patient. Similarly, adolescents are much more reluctant to discuss sex openly if they feel that their parents are uncomfortable with the topic. Consequently, to maximize your success, it is essential to open any dialogue at *your* level of comfort. If you begin to discuss sex with your child at a level that is obviously distressing to you, he may find it difficult to ask questions or to speak openly, and more than likely he will be reluctant to approach you with further inquiries. However, if you seem reasonably comfortable and make yourself accessible, you become a valuable resource for your child.

Therefore, one of the keys to successfully educating your adolescent about sex is a thorough understanding of your own level of comfort surrounding sexual communication.

This does not necessarily have any relationship to your own level of sexual fulfillment in your life. Many parents who are not happy with their own sexual situation are quite comfortable in passing along information that will help to protect their teenagers from the same fate. On the other hand, many parents who are comfortable and pleased with their own sexuality nonetheless find it hard to talk about sex with their teenagers.

To assess your personal level of comfort in discussing sexuality with your adolescent, take a piece of paper and fold it in half. On the left-hand side, write eight statements that represent the messages you would like to convey to your child about sexuality at this time. Don't worry about being consistent. You may find that you have statements as incompatible as "I want to give him permission to be sexual prior to marriage" and "I want him to hold off being sexual until after he is married." Simply write down the eight major messages you would like to convey without regard to consistency.

The first three to five statements may be fairly easy to think of, but it will probably take some deliberation to come up with eight. Nonetheless, concentrate until you have thought of all eight.

After you have completed this exercise, visualize yourself discussing each of these topics, one at a time, with your teen. Visualize your part of the discussion as well as his. Also, imagine the expression on each of your faces. When you're done, put two check marks in the left hand margin next to those topics you felt totally comfortable with, put one check next to those you were somewhat comfortable with, and none next to those you felt uncomfortable about. Be honest with your assessment. This is not a contest. There is no more virtue in having eight check marks than there is in having none. This is strictly a means of determining a beginning comfort level for you, so that when you feel ready to approach your adolescent, you know which issues you are prepared to deal with.

Determining *When* to Begin a More Intensive Sex Education

As I've mentioned, sex education is an ongoing process, not a one-shot deal. Your teenager is learning from your actions and from your words, from what is said as well as what is not said. Although most of his sex education has been unstructured and informal, your child has been receiving some education about the facts of life. One of these days you will start to suspect that your child needs substantially more sex information than you have thus far provided, and you will ask yourself, "Has the time come?"

It really is impossible to know precisely when your child is ready for sex information. It's not like sticking a toothpick into a cake and seeing if it's ready to come out of the oven. Such frequently used indicators as an adolescent's age or physical maturity are not very reliable. Even using your own experience as a teenager as a guideline may be misleading.

Teenagers today mature physically at an earlier age than we did. One controversial survey reports that women in Western Europe in the 1840s began their initial menstrual period at approximately age seventeen but that the age of menarche has consistently declined over the years. There is no question, in any case, that today's average age, a little under thirteen, is younger than in previous generations.[1]

Unfortunately, however, there is no evidence that this acceleration in physical maturity has been accompanied by a corresponding growth in emotional maturity. Moreover, children are individuals and mature at different rates. Some

18

twelve-year-olds may have the physical appearance and the drives of a fifteen-year-old and yet retain the emotional and intellectual development of a twelve-year-old. For a parent trying to figure out what to do, this can be confusing and even scary. Do you treat him like a fifteen-year-old? Or a twelve-year-old? Or do you bury your head in the sand and pretend that he is not maturing sexually? It would be comforting to have rules to go by, but the guidelines for parents are often ambiguous.

When it comes to giving your teenager sex information, it is impossible to pick the precise age or level of emotional maturity at which to begin this education. If you have been able to establish an open dialogue with your child, you will get *some* clues; if you're sure you can accurately assess his needs or believe that he will always come to you at the right time, you are either very fortunate or very naive.

Even the most open teenagers usually have difficulty talking to their parents about sex. Or, even if they feel very comfortable talking with one or both parents, their questions about birth control or sexually transmitted diseases will often come *after* their first intimate sexual experience. That may already be too late for the information they need.

Since it is virtually impossible to determine when your child is exactly ready for the sex information you need to impart, *talk to him at an age that is earlier than you think is necessary.* That doesn't mean that you should start teaching a five-year-old about intercourse. It simply means that you should not underestimate your adolescent's capacity to at least understand the factual aspects of sexuality, even if he may not understand the emotional context.

Think about what information you feel your adolescent will need in a year or two. *That is the information he needs to know right now.* If you give your child the information you judge him to be ready for today, there is a good chance that he has already passed that stage or will do so shortly.

19

The fact is that parents notoriously underestimate their adolescents' sexuality. In a famous 1979 survey of teenagers, Aaron Hass, Ph.D., asked whether teenagers felt their parents knew the extent of their sexual experience. "Only 28 percent of the boys and 25 percent of the girls replied Yes. . . . One of the most common explanations by teenagers for this state of affairs was the repeated observation that sex was simply not talked about in the home. In addition to this conspicuous silence, adolescents frequently sensed parents' desires to deny their maturation and sexual awareness."[2]

When asked "What kinds of things about your own sex life do you tell your parents?" the teenagers surveyed replied as follows:[3]

Boys	*Girls*	*Reply*
45%	51%	I only talk in a general way about sex, not specifically about me.
26	23	I tell them nothing about my sex life.
20	15	I tell them only what they would approve of.
9	11	I tell them almost everything.

In other words, only 10 percent of teenagers are telling their parents the full extent of their sexual activity.

3

UNDERSTANDING THE OBSTACLES

By parental standards, most teenagers are crazy. One day they are adults who want to enjoy a lack of responsibilities, like children; the next, they are children who want the privileges of adults. Adolescents are caught in a schizophrenic time warp, one minute feeling and acting like children, and the next like adults. They feel crazy, and we feel crazy in dealing with them. Sometimes we can't wait till they grow up, and sometimes this seems to be happening too quickly. Yet despite such inner turmoil, we expect them to be reasonable, and they expect the same from us; we want them to listen to us and to obey, and they want to be able to do what they feel like.

Humorist Bill Cosby describes our frustration in trying to communicate effectively with our adolescent children:

Nothing is harder for a parent than getting your kids to do the right thing. There is such a rich variety of ways for you to fail: by using threats, by using bribery, by using reason, by using example, by using blackmail, or by pleading for mercy. Walk into any bus terminal in America and you will see men on

21

benches poignantly staring into space with the looks of generals who have just surrendered. They are fathers who have run out of ways to get their children to do the right thing, for such a feat is even harder than getting my daughter to remember her own telephone number.[1]

The Inevitable Conflict

There is no doubt that dealing with teenagers can be a difficult and frustrating task. Yet it is important to keep in mind that in any conflict there must be at least two combatants and at least two perspectives. The conflict we experience in raising and educating our teenagers is no exception.

Certainly adolescents can be rebellious, and of course they feel a great deal of turmoil in their lives. That is a part of adolescence. However, it is important that as a parent you look at the role you play in the inevitable parent–teenager conflict. As noted child psychologist Haim Ginott points out, this conflict is basic to *all* parent–child relationships: "As parents our need is to be needed; as teenagers their need is not to need us. This conflict is real; we experience it daily as we help those we love become independent of us."[2] Adolescence can be a tug-of-war: we tug just as strongly as our teenagers do, especially when we attempt to get them to do what we want. Often it takes on the characteristics of a win-or-lose situation, where for one person to feel he has gotten what he wants, the other must feel as though he has lost.

Rather than blaming the inevitable parent–adolescent conflict on the teenager and perceiving the situation as one that he alone has created, it is critical that the parent look at the problem as one created by both the parents and the child.

As much as we may want to believe that our values and our perception of the world are the correct ones, it is important to respect that your kids also have opinions, thoughts, feelings, attitudes, and values. The fact that they play their music louder than you enjoy it, or the fact that the lyrics they derive pleasure from seem somewhat unintelligible, does not mean that their brains have turned to mush. It simply means that they have a different view of the world.

"That's Not What I Said"

I'm sure you can think of many instances when your child (or for that matter your spouse or a friend) refers to something that you supposedly told him, and your first words are, "That's not what I said!" Then he blasts back, "Yes it is! I heard you! You said . . ." And at that point he recites something that sounds vaguely familiar, but not at all how you intended it.

This is an example of a communication problem. The message you intended to communicate is received by your child in a somewhat different form. In any true communication between two people, there are two elements: a sender of the message and a receiver of the message. In a relatively simple communication, such as a personal letter, one party writes the letter (the sender) and one party reads the letter (the receiver). If the letter is precise, and if the receiver understands what the sender says, a clear communication has taken place. Yet even the most seemingly straightforward letter is subject to misinterpretation or "reading between the lines." In personal interactions, where every movement of the body and every expression of the face convey a message, the communication process is very complex. Consequently, what is received is often not exactly what was intended by the sender. A communication has taken place, but not an accurate one. Even under the best of circumstances, communications frequently get distorted.

Sex and Communication

As a society, we Americans are uncomfortable about sex. We laugh about it, whisper about it, and tell jokes about it, but rarely are we direct and open about it. When we curse, the words we use are often sexual in nature. Sex is a highly emotionally charged subject, and it is this emotion that makes the process of communication so difficult.

If sex wasn't so emotionally charged, would you be reading this book right now? After all, would you read a book about how to teach your child the rules of football, or how to teach the intricacies of cooking? Those are both very complicated subjects. You might read a book to help *yourself* understand those topics, but chances are slim that you would read a book about how to approach someone on the topic of cooking or about the subtleties of communicating about football. They are nonemotional subjects.

The fact is that our emotions color our communications. They distort our ability to send a precise message and our ability to listen with accuracy. The following paragraphs provide some examples of typical communication problems between parents and children. Although adolescents certainly deserve their share of the responsibility for such miscommunication, all the examples relate to poor parental communication. They are not intended to be an exhaustive list of communication problems between parents and their teenagers, nor are they meant to criticize you as a parent for making these types of mistakes. Rather, they are included to point out the importance of communication in the sex education process and the subtle (and not so subtle) ways in which we, as parents, sometimes interfere with that process. Only if you understand your participation in the parent–adolescent conflict can Chapter 6, "A Quick Primer on Communicating with Your Teenager," be used as an effective tool in improving such interactions.

Communication problems between parents and teenagers often arise because both feel uncomfortable in dealing with the subject of sex. Yet despite their discomfort, many parents feel an obligation to say *something*; then, instead of preparing for the opportunity, they quickly discharge what they perceive to be their "duty" at some inopportune moment and in an awkward way. Consequently, what comes out often communicates a message that was never intended:

> Stacy herself had learned about sex from her mother, in a supermarket, in the feminine-hygiene section. "There is a certain thing that adults do after they are married," Mrs. H. told her. "The purpose is to have children." She went on to explain the sexual process in such cold, clinical terms that Stacy's first question was, "Does a doctor perform the operation?"
> "No," said Mrs. H., "your father and I did it ourselves."[3]

Another common problem is that parents don't realize that even in their silence they send a message. The adolescent receives his education while the parent never realizes that much more has been communicated than was intended. Again, the example of Stacy's mother makes the point well:

In the years that followed, Mrs. Hamilton never mentioned the subject again. Not even a word. Stacy's mother seemed to consider sex an unmentionable obligation performed in unspeakable situations.[4]

Some miscommunications are two-sided. In the following example the parent communicated his unrealistic expectations to his sixteen-year-old daughter, and she intentionally deceives him in order to maintain her image in his eyes:

> I can't talk to my father at all, which is mostly due to the fact that I'm his only daughter. He thinks I'm the sweetest most virginal creature on earth and that I'm somehow sworn to eternal celibacy. I just go along with it and play the part.[5]

Sometimes what gets communicated either directly or indirectly by the parent is "I don't want to know anything about what is going on":

> I cannot even mention the word sex to my father—he'd throw a fit.[6]

> My mother once said if I ever needed birth control I should get it, but that she didn't want to know about it.[7]

Unfortunately, this "hands off" policy shuts down channels of communication and is often interpreted by the teenager to mean "You can do what you want as long as you keep it a secret." The net result is that the parent is cut off as a potential resource.

Often we hear of a "lack of communication" between adults and teenagers. Rarely is this the case. There is an abundance of communication between most adolescents and their parents; some verbal, most nonverbal. The only "lack" is of accurate communication. The messages that often get communicated are not at all what are intended. Evaluate not only what you intend to communicate but also what you do communicate with your words, your actions, and your lack of words and actions.

4

METHODS OF
SEX EDUCATION

Not all parents have the same skills in dealing with their teenagers, nor do all possess an equivalent level of knowledge about sex. Likewise, not all teenagers are responsive to the same types of parental input. This chapter is geared to help you assess all the resources available to you and how to use them most effectively.

Every parent–child relationship is unique. Thus, there is no single "right way" to educate your teenager about sex. The methods you choose to employ should be tailored to reflect your unique attributes as well as those of your adolescent. There is, however, one "wrong way" to approach your teenager's sex education: to say and do nothing to increase his knowledge about sex.

Every parent is capable of giving every adolescent an adequate sex education. There are no guarantees that he will use the information you provide for him; but to ignore the topic completely is to leave him vulnerable to myths and misinformation. In today's world, that can be fatal. As this chapter clearly shows, even in the most combative of parent–teenager relationships, it is possible to provide an adequate sex education.

Using Books

Books are the one method of teaching about sexuality that is an absolute necessity for virtually all teenagers. Even if your preference is to use one of the other methods listed, it is imperative that your teenager have at least one book about sex available to him.

Ideally, your child should be given one or more books about sexuality written specifically for teenagers. Many books about sexuality are written to accommodate the interests of parents and teachers, as well as teenagers. These books are likely to contain a great deal of information that is either irrelevant to the adolescent or written in a style that is uninteresting to him. Adolescents, like adults, will quickly discard any written material not geared to their level and their interests. So be certain that whatever books you provide are at your child's reading level and are written for and about adolescents. Since the interests and needs of teenage boys are considerably different from those of teenage girls, give priority to books that are written specifically for young men or young women.

Above all, be realistic. Teenagers are much more interested in the emotional and physical aspects of sex than they are in the intricacies of reproduction. Don't burden them with an old textbook about how babies are conceived and born. It probably won't get read. There are a number of excellent books available, written specifically for an adolescent, that cover the mechanics as well as the information necessary to protect his life and enhance his sexual growth, without turning him off.

As already discussed, it is a rare teenager who is willing to be completely open with his parents about his sexuality. Therefore it is doubtful that most adolescents will be willing to request specific sex information at the time they need

29

it. For this reason it is imperative that adolescents have information available to them on a constant basis.

If possible, give your child one or more books for his permanent use to keep in his room. Without a doubt, the first thing he will say is, "Leave me alone, I don't need that stuff, I know all of that already." Just tell him that's fine, but to browse through the book when he has a chance. *Do not order him to read the book.* Teenagers rarely respond to being forced into anything. If he says he doesn't want it in the room because his friends might see it, encourage him to keep it wherever he is most comfortable. Again, do not force the issue. Probably 90 percent of parents I have suggested this to have reported that within one week the book mysteriously disappeared from the shelf where the teenager placed it. Adolescents are very curious about sex, but they seem to have an unwritten code that it is "uncool" to look too anxious to get their hands on some written material.

The following excerpt from *A Young Woman's Guide to Sex* illustrates the point:

> Throughout my adolescence I was curious about sex, but in no way did I want anyone to know how curious I was. I sometimes spent hours skimming through novels from my parents' bookcase, looking for a few steamy scenes. Once I stayed up all night reading a boring novel because when I asked my dad if it was a good book he yelled *"No!"* From the tone of his voice I was sure it had some "hot" passages.
>
> Another book I found on my parents' shelf was a *Reader's Digest* medical guide. The book was *huge*, literally weighing five pounds, and had a bright green cover. I smuggled this thing up to my room (which is not easy to do with a five pound, bright green book) and hid in my closet with it. When I opened the book most of the words were in Latin and beyond figuring out anyway. For years I pretty much alternated between feel-

ing like a nerd for not knowing much about sex and feeling like a pervert for trying to find out about it.[1]

Giving your child a book about sex accomplishes two key things. First of all, and possibly most important, it implicitly gives him permission to experience sexual thoughts and feelings. By giving him a book you are saying, "It is OK for you to think about sex and to be curious about it." He will not have to feel "like a pervert for trying to find out about it." Second, by giving him a book, and permission to think about sex, he no longer needs to feel "like a nerd for not knowing much about sex." He now has the facts available to him on an "as needed" basis. If he is curious about intercourse, he can read the chapter about it. If he reads about AIDS or condoms in the newspapers, the book is available as a supplement. Whenever *he* feels the need to know more, such information is readily available.

If you choose not to buy a book for your teenager's permanent use, check one out for him from the library. Make sure that before the book is returned to the library you write down the name, author, and call number for him, and let him know which library it came from. He may protest when you write down the information for him, but tell him to put it in a drawer in case he needs it for further reference. Be aware, however, that your teenager will be much less likely to go to a library to seek out necessary sex information than he is to pick up a book from his own bookshelf. Consequently, making a library book available is a distant second choice to having a permanent copy available in your home.

The bibliography lists a number of books about sex written on specific topics or for certain age groups. Beginning on page 228 are the titles of a selection of books written specifically for teenagers. All the books referred to in the bibliography are fine books. Some will fit your needs and your teenager's more than others. Perhaps a combination of two or more books may be even more suited to your situation.

Although providing your child with appropriate reading material gives him the constant availability of needed information, what it does not give him is a person to talk to. A book cannot provide the interaction that he may need in order to discuss personal issues, nor does it necessarily furnish any resources if he has any problems or questions (although some of the books presented in the bibliography do list additional resources and explain how your child can avail himself of them). Ideally, books on sex education should be used as an adjunct with other, more personal methods of communication. This will give your teenager the best of both worlds.

Realistically, however, there are situations in which parents do not feel that personal communication about sex education is possible. This may occur in extreme cases where the teenager is so rebellious that he tends to oppose all parental communication, where the parent is so uncomfortable with the subject of sex that he or she would rather avoid talking about it, or where parent–teenager communication has deteriorated to the point that the parent chooses not to communicate. In these situations the parent should hand the teenager one or more books, following the advice above. In addition, the parent should recognize that this block in the relationship is an indication of serious personal or family problems, and professional counseling should be sought.

The Sex Lecture vs. The Discussion

As noted in chapter 1, The Sex Lecture, by itself, is a fairly ineffective method of conveying information about sex. The very term "lecture" points to its weakness. A lecture is a discourse given by one person to an audience. If you set yourself up as the lecturer, with your child as the audience, no dialogue is encouraged. Your child may absorb some important information, but at the same time some important questions may not get asked or answered.

Contributing to the weakness of this method is the fact that sex is an extremely complicated and emotionally charged subject. As already noted, even an expert on the subject could not communicate all that is necessary in one lecture or even a series of lectures. Rather than lecture about sex, try to encourage a discussion. Not only will this give you and your teenager a chance to exchange information, but if done according to the rules of good communication (see chapter 6), it tells your child that you are available if he should have questions or problems later, or even if he simply needs someone to listen.

The Ongoing Education

Probably the most effective method of sex education is that in which a dialogue is set up between parent and child and discussions about sex become a natural and normal part of conversation. In this way, either the parent or the teenager can feel free to bring up topics for discussion at any time. Of course, to establish such a free-flowing exchange, sex must be treated as naturally as discussions about the weather.

Setting up such a dialogue is not as difficult as you might think. There are a multitude of opportunities to discuss sex every day. Newspapers, magazines, TV, and movies can provide you with numerous opportunities to open a discussion about AIDS, teenage pregnancy, condoms, infidelity (in politics and otherwise), sex and religion, new breakthroughs in artificial fertilization, improvements or hazards in birth control devices, sexually transmitted diseases, and various other topics. Likewise, advertisements are common for sanitary napkins, tampons, feminine hygiene sprays, and now for condoms. Each of these sources represents an opportunity to provide your adolescent with more information. Each can lead to a discussion, and every discussion lets your child know that sex is an open topic.

5

THE RODNEY DANGERFIELD FACTOR: EVERYBODY NEEDS RESPECT

Even more important than *what* you teach your adolescent about sex is *how* you teach it to him. No matter how important the information you have, and how well organized it is, the information is worthless to your teenager until he has received it, absorbed it, and understood it. Achieving all of this is not an easy task.

This chapter and the one that follows are about how to communicate and convey information to your teenager and, equally important, how *not* to communicate with him. Obviously, my suggestions are not fail-safe. There are no guarantees that they will get your teenager to absorb the knowledge that you have to offer. The only guarantee is that if you do not recognize the critical importance of *how* to communicate effectively, much of your child's sex education will be lost.

Even under the best of circumstances and with the easiest of topics, communicating effectively with a teenager is difficult. They are moody, rebellious, cocky, self-centered, self-conscious, insecure, and often they feel they know all there is to know about any given topic. That's on their good days! Add to that the fact that they often view their parents as unknowledgeable (that's a polite term for "dumber than a toad"), old-fashioned, naive, and somewhat odd, and you do not have the makings of an easy exchange of information.

The Power Struggle

The fastest way to get an adolescent to ignore what you have to say is by treating him with a lack of respect. Actually, in many encounters, both the parent and the teenager feel they are treated with a lack of respect. This is often the core problem in many parent–adolescent interactions, as well as the reason that many parents and teenagers keep their interactions to a minimum.

In the typical scenario the teenager feels he is being treated like a child and in return treats the parent with disrespect. From there, a power struggle evolves. The parent, wanting to be treated with respect, tries to *control* the teen's mouth and behavior, and the teen, not wanting to be controlled, acts more rebellious and defiant. Each one is saying "I want to be respected" but is acting in a way that is continually more controlling and less respectful.

Teenagers seem to crave respect in three important areas:

1. Respect for their desire to feel independent from adults and to be able to act independently.
2. Respect for their opinions and values.
3. Respect for their privacy.

It is extremely important that in reading this you in no way confuse an adolescent's need for respect with an obligation on your part to agree with him. You are bound to disagree with many of the acts and ideas that your adolescent feels confident about. You can freely verbalize your disagreement and even your disapproval and still not do it in a way that is demeaning to your child.

Respecting Their Desire to Feel Independent

Whether you like it or not, in many ways your adolescent is an independent being. Certainly there are rules that you must enforce to keep your household running smoothly and to protect him from life-threatening consequences. However, don't expect your adolescent to agree with the rules or to appreciate them. Teenagers like to fancy themselves as free spirits.

As a way of emphasizing that they are independent, and to prove that you really have no control over them, teenagers rebel. Some do it visually, through their clothing or the way they groom themselves. Some do it verbally, by disagreeing with everything you say or through their tone of voice. Some do it quietly, going along with you, then doing what they want behind your back. Some do it in ways that seem annoying but not dangerous, whereas some threaten their lives or futures by using drugs, alcohol, sex, violence, crime, or failing at school to make their declaration of independence. The fact is, in one way or another, all adolescents rebel.

It is essential to understand that the more you try to eliminate their rebellion or attempt to control their behavior, the more you encourage them to rebel. The more they feel controlled, the less independent they feel; therefore the more they have to rebel in order to prove to you and to themselves that they are independent. It is a ritual that all teenagers go through.

The most important—and difficult—thing you must understand when you begin your teenager's formal sex edu-

37

cation is that *you cannot control your teenager's sexual behavior!* As much as you want him to respect your wishes, and as much as you want to protect him from his own ignorance, arrogance, and sexual drives, you cannot do it through *control.* The only exception to this is when your child's behavior becomes so erratic that it requires psychiatric hospitalization.

As an example, you cannot control whether your daughter gets pregnant. You can give her the knowledge to use the proper contraception, or you can erase some of the myths that might result in an accidental pregnancy. You might share some of your opinions and moral values about having intercourse at her age. But you cannot prevent her from getting pregnant. That is a choice that she will ultimately make.

Respect and control are not the same thing. Treat your adolescent with the same respect that you would an adult when talking to him about sex. Do not attempt to control his sexual behavior. If you disagree with a decision he has made, let him know that you disagree and share any consequences you may fear for him, but emphasize that the decision and the consequences are both his.

In situations that threaten your adolescent's safety or well-being, rules and limits are necessary, of course. But before you set any rules, be sure you are willing to enforce the consequences. Do not make idle threats. If necessary, write the rules down on paper; you and your teenager should sign the document, as you would a legal contract.

Respecting Their Opinions and Values

As a confident adult, I regard my view of the world as the correct one. After all, if I didn't believe my opinions and values were the right ones, I would change them. However, when dealing with other people it is important I accept that their view of the world is just as valid—*for them.* That doesn't mean I have to agree with their opinions or values, nor does it mean that they must agree with mine. It simply means that I must realize that my perception of the world, and the set of values and opinions I adopt as my own, are not the only valid ones in the world. Adolescents deserve the same respect. You may not agree with their opinions or values, but you must respect their right to think for themselves.

Whether they verbalize them or not, teenagers have a variety of opinions about sex. Some they absorb from what you have taught them or from sources that you feel are reliable; some result from peer pressure or from years of being blitzed by the media. Some are simply based on rebellion. It is unlikely that your adolescent's opinions about sex will mirror your own.

Respect the teenager's right to his own opinion. It is fine to disagree, but never ridicule his beliefs. If you challenge a teenager's beliefs by putting him down or demeaning him, you will not change his perceptions. All you will accomplish is to have him close off and hide his thoughts from you.

Opinions and Values Are Not Facts

One problem that parents often experience when they educate their children about sex is that they frequently confuse opinions and facts. If you tell your child "a girl may become pregnant if she engages in intercourse," that is a fact. If you say that it is "good" or "bad" for her to engage in intercourse, that is your opinion.

Parents are certainly entitled to pass on their opinions and their moral values to their children, but it is important that these not become confused with facts. Each requires a somewhat different form of communication. No matter how convinced you are that your opinions and moral values are the "correct" ones, be aware that they still are not facts. The more certain you are of their correctness, the more danger there is that you may confuse them with facts.

Recognize the difference between the facts and the opinions you present. When you do express an opinion or a moral value, preface it with the statement that this is your *personal belief. Do not try to convince your adolescent that your opinions are right or that his are wrong.* If he differs with you on a moral matter or on an opinion, just ask that you be heard out, and give him the same respect. Do not mock his opinions. He may be just as convinced as you are that his values are the correct ones, or he may differ with you just to be oppositional. In either case, it is very doubtful that you will shake him loose from his point of view. Don't be afraid to let him know how passionately you feel about your position and how strongly you disagree with him. Realize that some of his opinions and moral values will be different from yours, and that the more control you try to exert over his moral values and opinions, the more he is likely to rebel or to shut you out. If he disagrees with you about some factual matters, find a book that can settle the dispute.

Adding to the confusion between opinions/beliefs and facts about sex is the misuse or abuse of terms like "normal" and "abnormal," "good" and "bad," "right" and "wrong," and sometimes even "healthy" and "unhealthy."

"Normal" is a statistical term meaning "usual." It is "normal" for people to put a sock on each of their feet and then put on both shoes, but occasionally someone likes to put on his left sock and shoe followed by his right sock and shoe. Even though this person might be considered "abnormal," because he doesn't do what is usual for most people, it does not mean he is sick, crazy, or weird.

Frequently the term "abnormal" is misused in a judgmental manner when people are uncomfortable about something. For example, it is not uncommon to hear parents talk about masturbation as "abnormal." Since surveys show a large majority of teenagers, both male and female, do masturbate, such behavior is statistically normal. What these parents mean to say is that they don't approve of masturbation. This certainly is their privilege, but it has nothing to do with normal or abnormal, healthy or unhealthy. What it has to do with is their personal beliefs. It is important that your teenager know what your values are.

However, be clear about what you mean. If you are at all judgmental, be explicit that you are stating an opinion. At the same time recognize your child's right to differ from you. Like a good attorney, a teenager will often twist your judgmental statements and then act as a jury and convict you of not understanding him.

As an exercise, take out the list that you made in chapter 2, and place an *F* next to those items on your list that are facts and an *O* next to those that are opinions or moral judgments. This will help you begin to recognize the difference between the two categories and will be important when you finally do start the process of formal sex education.

Respecting Their Privacy

We all have a need for privacy. *Teens need uninterrupted time, a place or room that they can feel is their space, possessions of their own, and the right to private thoughts and fantasies.* As parents we want to respect their privacy but we also want to be included in their lives and to know as much as possible about what they are doing (both out of curiosity and for their protection).

Many teenagers resent their parents' asking too many questions yet feel equally resentful if their parents show no interest or curiosity at all. In a sense, it's a no-win situation. Don't try to make sense out of it. Part of your teenager wants the independence that he perceives you to have as an adult, and part of him needs to know that you care enough to be there still.

Do not confuse privacy with secrecy. Privacy is simply the need to experience an event without the presence of another person to clutter or invade the experience. Secrecy stems from a desire to hide, often from a sense that what you are doing is evil or shameful.

Let your children know that you are available to them if they want to share things with you. If you have a concern, tell them and ask any questions that you think are appropriate, but be prepared for the fact that your teenager may not want to share much information with you. If your teenager's reaction gives you the feeling that you are intruding on his territory, clearly let him know that your intention is not to be an intrusion but to be a resource.

If you want to earn your teenager's respect, keep in mind that this is a two-way street. To gain respect you must give respect. If you practice the principles I have outlined here, you can maintain an open flow of communication. If you fail to give your teen respect, effective communication will be difficult and laborious, if not impossible.

6

A QUICK PRIMER ON COMMUNICATING WITH YOUR TEENAGER

There is no doubt that good communication in any relationship, whether it be with a child, a spouse, or a friend, is an extremely valuable asset. When it comes to providing your adolescent with a sex education, good communication can certainly open doors that are closed to parents whose relationship with their teenagers is strained. But no matter how difficult communication may be between you and your teen, an adequate sex education *can* be provided. *The level of communication between the two of you will not determine whether you can give your child a sex education. It will only dictate in what manner that education can best be provided.*

The goal of this chapter is to teach you the basic rules of effective communication. However, no matter how much time you take to understand these guidelines, and no matter how conscientious you are about implementing them, there will be times when communication between the two of you breaks down. When this occurs, simply recognize your role in the breakdown, so that next time you can improve the process. *Do not condemn yourself because you are not perfect.*

43

Understanding What You Have
Communicated about Sex

One point of crucial importance that has already been made is that not all communication takes place on a verbal level. When you speak to someone, much more is communicated than just your words. The tone of your voice, your facial expression, a gesture, a touch, or even the position of your body can change the meaning of what you say. With a subject as emotionally charged as sex, these extra cues often speak louder than any words.

Even not saying a word can communicate a message. For instance, if your teenager says nothing to you about sex, you may interpret that to mean "I am not interested in sex" or "I know all I need to know about sex." Likewise, a parent's silence might be interpreted as "Sex is a forbidden subject" or "My parent doesn't care what I do."

The fact is that you have been communicating with your teenager about sex. The question is, are you aware of *what* you have been communicating? The following exercise is designed to help you evaluate what messages about sex and sex education you and your adolescent have communicated to each other. Its purpose is simply to make you aware of the constant flow of communication that you exchange with your teenager.

Take out the list of messages you prepared in chapter 2. Now, on the right-hand side, next to each statement you listed, write the messages you feel you have actually communicated about that issue. Don't forget to consider what you have communicated through nonverbal messages or through any books or other educational materials you have made available to your teen. Now compare each of the messages you previously listed with what you feel has been communicated. This is not a test. There is no score. It is simply an exercise to help you compare the messages about sex you have been communicating with the messages you want to communicate.

Understanding the Basic Rules of Communication

Now that you have an idea about what you have been communicating, let's take a look at the basics of effective and ineffective communication. I believe that an understanding of basic communication skills will enable you to make this process between you and your adolescent more effective.

Effective Listening

There are two basic parts to effective communication, sending and receiving. Ordinarily, you might refer to these two aspects as speaking and listening. However, since much communication takes place nonverbally, try to think of it more broadly. Most people seem to recognize the importance of the sending or speaking aspects of communication, but unfortunately the listening aspect is often devalued.

Listening effectively in a conversation about sex is often not an easy task. Sex is such an uncomfortable subject in our society that both parents and teens frequently find it difficult to listen effectively. In a survey done by Aaron Hass, adolescents were asked "Have you ever tried to talk openly with either of your parents about sex? If you have tried, how did they respond?" The results of his survey indicate that "the common parental responses reported by teenagers were teasing, denial, and . . . punishment." Very often, a teenager felt lectured at instead of listened to.

"Some teenagers proudly reported parental responses indicating interest, understanding, and reassurance. These adolescents felt safe while talking with their parents, and more importantly, believed their feelings and views were heard and not simply judged."[1]

Rule 1. If you are talking to your adolescent about sex (or any other topics of importance), attend to what he is saying, shut off any other distractions, and make eye contact with him. If the time is inconvenient, set up an alternative time when both of you will be able to listen effectively. Likewise, if you initiate a conversation with him, pick a time when he is not otherwise distracted.

The way in which you listen to your teen can critically affect the way he responds in a conversation. Continuing to watch TV or read a newspaper while he talks, checking your watch, yawning, or just generally looking as though you would rather be somewhere else—all communicate disinterest and will give him little incentive to continue opening up. On the other hand, if you look at him and genuinely seem to be engaged in the conversation, he is more likely to share his thoughts and feelings. Ultimately, the way in which you demonstrate that you are listening will greatly affect the success of your interactions.

Rule 2. Let your teenager know that you are listening attentively by occasionally clarifying what you have heard. Clarifying can be helpful in two ways. First, it can assure your teenager that you have listened to and understood what he has said. Second, it gives him the opportunity to restate his remarks if it turns out that there is a misunderstanding.

The best way to clarify is to briefly summarize, in your own words, what you believe he is saying. For instance, if you were trying to clarify what I have said so far in this section, you might say "What you are saying to me, then, is that listening effectively is a very important part of the communication process. And that by listening carefully and clarifying what is being said, I can improve the quality of my interactions." I'd respond "Exactly!" and we would know that we understand each other. If I thought that you misunderstood me, or missed an important point, I might say "Not exactly" and try to again explain so that we could clear up the confusion.

Rule 3. Show your teen that you want to know what's on his mind by listening to him without interruption. Interrupting him before he has a chance to complete his thought indicates a lack of respect. And, as discussed, teens are very sensitive to the issue of respect. Besides, no one likes to be interrupted.

Methods of Sharing Information

Before you consider the effective methods of sharing information with your teenager, it is important to understand the methods that are most ineffective. Again, as a living and breathing parent, there are going to be times when you "slip" and use some of these ineffective methods. However, with some awareness of what you are doing, and a conscious effort to eliminate destructive communication, you can maximize your effectiveness.

Such negative forms of communication as pressuring, punishment, embarrassment, teasing, criticism, shock, and rejection have one thing in common. They make the teenager feel bad about himself or his actions. And, as a result, one or more of the following consequences is likely to occur:

1. The teenager will become reluctant to share his feelings and thoughts.
2. He will feel fear, shame, or guilt (which may persist for years or even throughout his lifetime).
3. The power struggle between the teenager and the parent will increase and open the door for rebellion.

Rule 4. When talking about matters of sexuality, use positive methods of communication. Negative forms will result in your being shut out from your teenager's life and may have long-lasting, damaging consequences for his maturation as a sexual being.

No matter how positive your interactions with your teenager have been, don't expect a lot of feedback when it comes to discussing sex. Teenagers are notoriously private about their sexuality. They tend to be so insecure about the subject that many will not even be honest about their thoughts and feelings with their closest friends. This is especially true of adolescent boys.

So don't feel personally affronted if your teenager seems to be in a hurry to leave the room when you bring up the topic of sex. Just try to maximize the situation's potential. There should definitely be a feeling of privacy. If both parents want to be there, fine, but don't choose a time when any of his friends or siblings are present. Make sure that sufficient time is available, so that no one feels rushed.

Start by picking the topic that you most want to address (check through your list before you start). Be clear on what you are trying to say, and be direct. If you want to talk to your son about pregnancy prevention and condoms, start with that. Don't begin with the birds and the bees, because by the time you get to the part about condoms, he'll have left the room.

Let him know from the start that if he has any questions, he can just fire away. And, again, answer the questions directly. Do not try to protect him from the truth. If you become indirect or evasive, you will lose your credibility, and everything you say or have said may be negated.

If he asks a question that you don't know the answer to, *don't guess.* Tell him that you will try to find out the answer for him. In that way you can provide him with accurate information, and, at the same time, it may allow you a second opportunity during which you can follow up with any information you failed to share the first time around.

Do not hesitate to share any concerns you may have for his safety, especially around such important topics as AIDS, other sexually transmitted diseases, or pregnancy. However, when you do so, make sure you implement the rules for effective communication.

Rule 5. When sharing your concerns or feelings, start your sentences with "I," or preferably "I feel (angry, glad, hurt, sad, etc.)." If you are threatening or accusatory, or start your sentences with "you," the other person is likely to become defensive and close the dialogue.

In my work as a clinical psychologist, one of the greatest impediments to clear communication that I encounter is the tendency for people to throw accusations at others, rather than sharing their own feelings. I very often hear statements like "You make me so angry when you . . ."

Think about that for a minute. If someone says to *you,* "You make me so angry . . . ," your most likely response is going to be to defend yourself, and then possibly to try to put him on the defensive. That inevitably deteriorates into a pitched battle rather than resulting in clear discussion of the issue.

The point is that beginning a sentence with the word "you" puts people on the defensive. If you start with "I," they tend to listen more effectively. (Starting a sentence, "*I* think that *you* . . ." is the same as starting with "you.") If your goal is effective communication, start your sentences with "I," followed by a feeling.

For instance, let's say you are concerned that your daughter is getting too emotionally involved with a boy and that she might become pregnant. Rather than say "You are getting too involved with that boy!" and risk her getting defensive, you might try "I am concerned about your involvement with Joe. I worry that you'll get so swept off your feet that you might be careless sexually and end up pregnant." The difference between the two statements is that in the first you are challenging her, and in the second you are merely stating your feelings. If your daughter still got defensive about the second statement, you could reply "I'm just telling you my concerns. I'm not saying it will happen; I just worry about you."

Rule 6. Always be clear in stating what you want. Many adults have a tendency to say what they do *not* want, rather than what they *do* want. Saying what you don't want is fine, as long as you are also clear about what you want.

For instance, saying to your teenager "I don't want you staying out so late at night" does not give him any clue as to what you do expect. A statement such as "I want you back by 1:00 A.M. on Friday and Saturday, and by 9:00 P.M. on all other nights" is much clearer about exactly what your expectations are.

Rule 7. Wherever possible, rephrase your questions as statements that reflect your feelings. Many times questions are used not to elicit information but to trap someone. For instance, you might say to your teenager: "Why don't you date other boys besides John?" In truth, you really don't care *why* she is not dating others. You are expressing your own displeasure, not asking what she thinks. No matter what she replies, you are going to argue with her.

Instead of asking that question, you might say "I think that a girl your age should not limit herself to one boyfriend. I would really like you to consider not restricting yourself." Notice that not only did I eliminate the use of a question, but I also incorporated "I" language and was direct about what I wanted.

Rule 8. When in any kind of disagreement, avoid the use of "absolutes" like "always," "never," "whenever," "every time," or any other statement that might drag up the past. Be very careful how you use these words when sharing your thoughts. No matter what you say, it will be met with a challenge. Invariably, when you throw an "absolute" at people, they manage to cite the one single time when the exception occurred.

If your teenager comes home late and you say "You are always coming home late," you can expect him to reply "That's not true; on a Thursday night last April, I came home on time." Then, what frequently happens is that you begin to argue about whether he really did come home on time on a Thursday night last April. The two of you get wrapped up in a battle that has nothing to do with the present. The point you were trying to make about his missing curfew this evening gets lost.

Most statements that drag up the past tend to divert you from dealing with the present. Many times people will use the past as "ammunition" to prove their point. Even a simple statement like "You came home late last week also" is enough to derail the point you are trying to make. Stick to the present if you want to make your point effectively.

If you feel some past event is unresolved, say so and talk about your present feelings about that incident. It is unnecessary to rehash every detail about what did or did not take place.

Obviously, good communication takes a lot of work. Often, we act as if everyone is born with the ability to communicate. However, effective communication is not an innate process. It is something we learn. And unless you have taken classes in communication skills, all of what you have learned about this complicated process has been through trial and error.

The rules presented in this chapter are deceptively simple. They are easy to understand and extremely effective when used consistently. By working diligently to implement them, you can significantly improve your interactions with your teenager, and possibly with other important people in your life as well.

II

WHAT YOUR TEENAGER
NEEDS TO KNOW

7

YOUR TEENAGER NEEDS
MORE THAN FACTS

Many parents wonder what it is exactly that they should
teach their adolescents about sex. What does your teenager
need to know about pregnancy? Or about AIDS? What are
the important facts that they absolutely have to know? This
section of the book covers all the critical medical information your teenager must have as well as the important
emotional and physiological aspects of sex. However, before dealing with the specifics of any of these subjects, it
is important to look at some of the intangible, unclassifiable
nuances of sexuality that must be addressed, aspects that
are rarely, if ever, considered, but which are absolutely
critical to your teenager if he is to mature into a healthy
sexual being.

Self-Esteem

Self-esteem is a critical component of an adolescent's sexual
maturation. It is difficult for a teenager to feel positive about
himself as a sexual being when low self-esteem deprives

him of the confidence to make contact with his peers. And once his self-esteem has eroded, it is difficult for him to state his feelings openly or to ask the questions that are so necessary to build an information base. On the other hand, insecurities about his sexuality, or feelings of guilt and shame, can damage his feelings of self-worth. It can be a never-ending cycle.

Parents play a crucial role in helping a teenager develop high self-esteem. Likewise, they can be just as instrumental in deflating a child's confidence. Your whole pattern of interactions with your child, beginning at birth, has an impact on his sexual development. So don't underestimate the importance of your everyday relationship with your child as a factor in his sexual development. Self-esteem is such a complex matter that we cannot exhaust the topic here. However, there is one rule of thumb that is extremely important in encouraging a teenager to feel good about himself. *People learn more effectively when they are praised for what they have accomplished than when they are criticized for what they have not accomplished. Avoid making remarks that are derogatory about your teenager. Instead, try to concentrate on giving him praise for his successes.*

Many good books are available that can help your child develop the self-esteem necessary to become a healthy sexual being. (See, e.g., under "Parenting," p. 228.) If you feel your adolescent is lacking in self-esteem, read one and try implementing some of its recommendations.

Giving Permission—A Balancing Act

Of all the gifts that a parent can bestow upon a teenager, possibly the most precious is permission to be a sexual person or, just as important, permission not to be sexually active. Teenagers get all sorts of mixed messages about whether they should be sexual. We live in a society that caters to sexual interests through blatantly erotic advertising and sexual innuendo on TV and in the movies. Yet the same media avoid open discussions about sex. The message these media send our teens is: it's OK to deal with sex in indirect ways but not to talk openly about it. We teach girls that the shape of their body and flirting are critical in attracting the male of their choice, but that if they are not very selective about how they exhibit their shape or if they are not careful about flirting, they can attract the wrong element and open themselves up for rape. Again, a mixed message: try to look attractive and sexy, but watch out if you do. Even as parents, we give them mixed messages, because we ourselves have ambivalent feelings about their sexuality. We want our teenagers to experience whatever is necessary for them to learn to enjoy their own sexuality. Yet there is a part of us that wants to protect them from the dangers that go along with sex and possibly even a part that is reluctant to see them grow up.

No wonder teenagers are confused. Their adolescent hormones say "Yes, be sexual," while they get conflicting messages from their friends, family, and society as a whole.

Just by letting your teenager know that it's natural for him to be interested in sex, and that his sexuality is a normal part of the maturation process, you can remove a tremendous burden from his shoulders. If Mom or Dad say it's OK to think about sex and to have sexual feelings toward others, this removes much of the confusion that has resulted from all the double messages our society sends.

Equally important, though, is giving your adolescent permission not to be a sexual person. For various moral, physical, or emotional reasons, many teenagers are not ready to be sexually active. Yet because of peer pressure, or even through unintended messages transmitted by their parents, they get the idea that it is expected of them to engage in some level of sexual activity. It is essential that when you give your child permission it be a two-way swinging gate; they should feel they have permission either to be sexually active or not to be sexually active.

Our basic instinct as parents is to protect our children. This applies to all aspects of their lives, including sex. Consequently, it is not unusual for a parent to list all the dangers and responsibilities that go along with being a sexually active person, and to forget to include the joys. It is extremely important that you present both sides to your teenager. To communicate *only* the positive, joyful aspects could lead to him adopting a naive, irresponsible, or even dangerous attitude, whereas expressing only the dangers and responsibilities can lead to unnecessary fear and anxiety.

Responsibility and Moral Values

The nature of your moral values will, to some degree, influence what you perceive to be your teenager's responsibilities in a sexual relationship. However, no matter what your moral beliefs are, there are at least three responsibilities that you *must* cover with your teenager: his responsibility to himself, his responsibility to his partner, and his responsibility to others his behavior may affect, such as any offspring that might result if a pregnancy occurs. It is essential for him to understand that sexual intimacy with a partner is not a game or a ritual that must be performed to pass into adulthood.

The basic responsibility your adolescent has to himself is to be aware of the potential consequences of what he is doing and to recognize that whatever the results, he is accountable. This means an awareness that, along with the joy of sex, there are potential life-altering consequences (AIDS, pregnancy, other sexually transmitted diseases, and so on).

This is extremely difficult for many teenagers to absorb. They seem to have a view of the world in which they see themselves as immortal and immune from the dangers of life. Often they fail to see the risk in their actions. This is why the largest cause of death among teenagers is accidents and why teenagers are projected to be at such great risk for contracting AIDS.

The second area of responsibility is also very difficult for teenagers to accept, particularly for teenage boys. For the most part, teenagers are very egocentric and self-absorbed. They tend not to consider the consequences for others. So it is very important to get across to your adolescent that he absolutely must respect his partner's rights. No one should be forced into sexual activity. Physical force, emotional arm twisting, and even the simple use of guilt or manipulation are all forms of coercion. Even if his relationship is a mutually consenting one, he has a responsibility to respect his partner's health and welfare. It is their shared responsibility to appropriately use contraception and avoid the transmission of sexually transmitted diseases.

Finally, teenagers need to understand that the potential consequences of irresponsible sex may be life altering not only for themselves and their partner but even for other family members. Sexually transmitted diseases, an unwanted pregnancy, abortion, or forced sex can entail a number of devastating medical, legal, financial, emotional, and moral problems, along with increased responsibilities.

A Listening Ear

As a parent, one important gift you can offer your teenager is the comfort of knowing that you are available for guidance and counseling any time he needs it, and that you are not going to sit in judgment and condemn him, no matter how much you may disagree with his choices. Even though teenagers rarely take full advantage of this parental counseling service, just the knowledge that you will be there when they need you adds a little comfort to the daily tensions of being a teenager.

8

PREPARATION FOR PUBERTY

Puberty is an extraordinary time for children and parents alike. By definition, it is the period when a child matures and becomes capable of reproduction. However, it is not only a time of change for a youth's body, but also it is a period when his mind, his perception of himself, and his perception of the world changes as well. Likewise, the parents' view of their child is altered, as they see the first signs of him developing into an adult. In one way or another, the relationship between a child and his parents is permanently changed during this phase.

Girls usually reach puberty between the ages of nine and fourteen, and boys between twelve and sixteen. The time of its onset is the result of hormonal changes within the body and, to a large degree, is determined by hereditary factors. There is nothing that you or your child can do to slow down this maturation process or to speed it up, although certain life-styles and medical conditions may delay its onset. For example, eating disorders that cause a teenager to be underweight or malnourished (such as anorexia) may cause puberty to be delayed. Similarly, vigorous athletic activity (such as long-distance running) may slow the process. Every child matures at his or her own rate.

Puberty officially begins for a male when his penis spurts forth the thick whitish fluid called semen; for a female, when she experiences her first menstrual period. However, for as much as a year or two before this momentous occurrence that declares your child an adolescent, his or her body has already gone through a number of preparatory changes. Consequently it is essential that you prepare both yourself and your child for puberty well before the event takes place.

For the parent looking for intimacy with his or her child, the information about puberty presents a golden opportunity. The parent who feels uncomfortable talking about this topic should note that all the following material, with one important exception, can be communicated by a good book. Both *A Young Man's Guide to Sex* and *A Young Woman's Guide to Sex* are recommended for this purpose. The only information that must be conveyed directly by the parent is that he or she is available at any time if the child has questions or needs to talk.

Puberty is a time of dramatic changes in a youth's body. For your child to endure these changes without any preparation or understanding can result in a great deal of unnecessary fear and serious confusion. On the other hand, if your child understands what to expect, this period is more likely to be experienced as a very exciting time.

The following reports evidence some typical fears that teenagers experience if they are not prepared for the dramatic changes of puberty.

> I was never told what it would feel like when my breasts started to grow and was convinced I had cancer.

The first few times I ejaculated was when I was asleep. Each time, when I woke up I thought I had urinated. I was so embarrassed that I hid my wet underclothes. I didn't know who to turn to. It was years later before I figured out that what I was going through was normal.

When my cousin started her period, she thought she had been raped in her sleep, because she thought the only way to start your period was after the first time you have sex.

The simplest way to deal with puberty is to explain to your child what is going to happen to his body. Be sensitive to the fact that he is still a child and will be scared by "horror stories" about what happened when Aunt Jane got her first period or Cousin Jake ejaculated. On the other hand, your information shouldn't be so indirect that it seems to have nothing to do with his own life.

The following is information that your adolescent needs to know. The facts about menstruation are important for both boys and girls to understand, although boys do not need quite as much of the detail.

The Growth Spurt and External Changes

As the hormonal pattern changes within the child, one of the most noticeable results is the "growth spurt." During this time your child will grow taller at a faster rate than ever before. Because the arms, legs, and hands sometimes lengthen even faster than the rest of the body, many adolescents experience a feeling of awkwardness. It is during this time of rapid growth that a boy's vocal cords stretch, often resulting in a "cracking" of his voice and a change in the depth of his tone. Most girls usually reach their final height by age sixteen, most boys by eighteen.

At about the same time that the body is lengthening, other very noticeable changes occur. Thick, coarse hair begins to grow around the genital area, and for boys, on the abdomen, chest, and face. The amount of hair is an inherited trait, so there is nothing they can do to change the growth pattern.

Breasts will begin to grow and protrude in girls. The appearance of these breast buds is often their first sign of puberty. Almost all girls feel that the growth in their breasts is too slow or too rapid, or that the size of their breasts is too small or too large. There is probably not an adolescent girl alive who would not change something about her breasts if she could, but like body hair, the size and shape of breasts are determined by heredity. Boys often experience a temporary enlarging of the breasts called gynecomastia (gine-eh-ko-mass-tee-a), which they may feel embarrassed about but which actually occurs in up to 80 percent of boys.

Similarly, the genitals begin to mature about this time. Boys will notice a lengthening of the penis, enlarging of the testes, and a reddening and wrinkling of the scrotum. They will begin to get more noticeable erections. Likewise, they will experience ejaculations, most often as a result of "wet dreams" or of masturbation. It is important, as the example on page 63 indicates, that a young boy understands that these nocturnal emissions are normal.

The breasts and the penis are very important symbols of sexuality for adolescents. Youngsters should know that the size of these organs has nothing at all to do with masculinity or femininity, sexual ability, intelligence, or any other significant trait.

Finally, in most adolescents, the body begins to produce an increase in skin oils, which clog pores and produce pimples and blackheads. Teenagers can minimize their acne by cleansing often and not picking at the pimples. If the acne becomes severe, medical attention should be sought.

Menstruation

Few events in our lives are so important that we can remember where we were when they occurred. For almost all women, their first menstrual period (menarche) is one of those events. Because of the tremendous emotional impact of this event, it is extremely important that your daughter be prepared to expect menstruation and to celebrate it as an exciting part of growing up.

Here are the experiences of two girls that reflect the enormous impact adequate preparation can have on your daughter:

I started my period the summer I was to become twelve years old and also a junior high school student! When I saw that I had drenched my underpants with blood, I literally fainted with worry that I was sick. I ran to Mom, and she gave me a diaper to wear. I mean literally a cloth baby diaper. She told me that for the rest of the week I was not to shower, run, wear heels, or think bad thoughts. She didn't explain the reason for the bleeding. For the next whole year, one week out of a month I lived with frustration, curiosity, and dirtiness. I hated whatever it was I was going through.

I hated Mom for not telling me about it. But I was afraid to ask.

At first I got scared when I saw the blood, but then I realized what was happening. My mother had let me know what to expect ever since I was nine. When I told her what was happening to me, she gave me a big hug. Later she and my dad came into my room and gave me a rose that they had picked. It was really a beautiful day.

The average age for menarche is twelve years old, although it may occur anywhere between ten and fifteen. Therefore most girls should be prepared from age eight as to what to expect. If a girl has not experienced her first period by sixteen, a physician should be consulted.

Some basic understanding of the physiological process behind the menstrual cycle can go a long way toward assuring a young woman that her periods are neither magical nor dirty. Girls need to know that periods are a result of their uterus shedding its lining, that menstruation will occur approximately monthly for the next thirty to forty years, and that this cycle is simply a biological fact of life.

In addition, they need to know that it is simply untrue that during their periods they cannot exercise, swim, take baths, and function as they normally do. In fact, bathing or showering can make them feel more comfortable and keep them from developing an unpleasant odor from the menstrual flow.

Their preparation should also include some instruction on how to use sanitary napkins or tampons. In fact, it is a good idea to supply your daughter with a kit of minipads or junior-sized tampons, in case you are unavailable when she begins her initial period.

Parents as well as adolescent girls should be aware of a condition known as Toxic Shock Syndrome. It is a rare but extremely dangerous disease, which seems to occur most frequently in young women during their menstrual periods. It has been associated with the use of tampons and possibly with menstrual sponges. The symptoms include a high fever, vomiting or diarrhea, and dizziness. Other possible symptoms are muscle aches, bloodshot eyes, sore throat, and a sunburnlike rash that may lead to peeling (especially on the hands and feet). If these symptoms show up, immediate medical treatment should be sought.

9

TOUCHING AND SEXUAL INTIMACY

Exploration is the most natural of all experiences for an infant. He investigates every object within his vicinity. He looks at it, listens to it, touches it, even tastes it if he is able. Naturally, since his own body and that of his parents are readily available, he treats them as he would any other object. He explores his fingers, his toes, his genitals, and every other nook and cranny of his body. Likewise, he may put his mother's fingers in his mouth, pull at her hair, or touch her breast. Everything is a source of wonder and amazement.

Each of us is born with the same inclination to touch and explore. However, at some early age we begin to learn that not all touching is appreciated or tolerated. We learn not to pull hair and not to touch our genitals in public (or not at all). We learn that some people like to be touched and others don't. Some learn that touching may result in a close bonding with another person, but others find that their touch causes their friends or family to pull away. We learn all this by trial and error, observation of those who are closest to us, and through the pressures of our society.

The point is that when a child is born, touching is a natural experience. It is through outside forces such as parental or societal pressures that this comfort with touching oneself or others becomes modified and inhibited. The more readily these early explorations are accepted by the parents or other adults in the environment, the greater the likelihood that the child will become comfortable with physical contact. As acceptance is decreased and punishment is increased, the more likely it is that the child will learn to refrain from these interactions.

Masturbation

Boys handle their penises every day when they urinate, so it is no great surprise that virtually every teenage boy quickly discovers that his penis is capable of sexual sensations when he enters puberty. Besides, teenage boys are constantly talking about sex and masturbation as if they were rights of passage into adulthood. Therefore virtually 100 percent of adolescent males will at least make some attempt to masturbate. Some will not continue all the way to ejaculation, and some will do it only once or twice, but virtually ALL teenage boys will try it out of curiosity.

Likewise, many young girls will discover the sexual sensations in their genitals while washing themselves, toweling themselves dry, climbing a tree, or just straddling a chair. Some will continue to stimulate themselves to orgasm, whereas others will in one way or another inhibit this practice.

According to a survey by Aaron Hass, in the age group from fifteen to sixteen, 75 percent of boys and 52 percent of girls said they masturbated. The figures increased to 80 percent of the boys and 55 percent of the girls for eighteen-year-olds.[1]

It will be helpful if you can let your teenager know, either through conversation or through a book, that masturbation is normal. Even if you have religious or moral objections, it would be helpful to acknowledge that it is natural for teenagers to be interested in exploring their own bodies, and then go on to explain your set of values about masturbation. Do not use guilt or shame as weapons. They tend not to eradicate behaviors but rather serve to drive them underground. Teenagers who are secretive about their sexuality, and who feel abnormal and guilty about the most natural of drives, will ultimately feel fear and confusion about their adult sexuality.

Parental concerns about masturbation are not a new phenomenon. One has only to go back a short time to when masturbation was so feared by parents that "remedies" bordered on physical torture.

> Some of the more extreme remedies involved tying boys' hands to their bedposts or chaining them to walls when they slept; putting a wire ring through the foreskin of the penis or wearing a spiked ring on the penis, both procedures making erection and stimulation extremely painful; the wearing of straightjacketlike restraints to keep the hands away from forbidden territory; and in a few cases, even castration [cutting off the testicles] and surgical removal of the penis.[2]

There are many myths about masturbation: that it causes pimples, stomach upsets, impotence, epilepsy, inability to conceive children, decreased athletic performance, growing of hair on the palms of the hand, or blindness. Obviously, all these are untrue. From the scientific standpoint, there are no indications that masturbation involves any physical or emotional dangers. Virtually all social scientists agree that masturbation is a natural form of sexual expression and that, other than the guilt inflicted by parental or societal admonitions, there is no danger.

Petting and Intercourse

Petting and intercourse are extremely difficult to talk to teenagers about in a constructive way. Once you have passed that difficult hurdle of accepting that the child whom you have raised from infancy is, or is going to be, a sexually intimate human being, there is a very delicate equilibrium that must be dealt with. That is the balancing act of painting a realistic picture of the responsibilities and dangers of sex, including pregnancy, rape, sexually transmitted diseases such as AIDS, and all the other potential tragedies of a sexual encounter, and yet letting him know that sexual intimacy can be wonderful under the right circumstances.

Unless you have a long leash, you cannot make sexual decisions for your teenager. When and under what circumstances he or she chooses to be sexually active are not under your direct control. There are, however, a number of issues that you may address that may help your teenager to decide what the right circumstances might be for him or her.

Avoiding Coercion

Teens need to understand that under no circumstances should they let themselves be coerced or manipulated into having intercourse. Probably from portrayals of sex in the movies, in novels, and on TV, a great many teens have gotten the idea that coercion and sex go hand in hand. The following startling survey of teenage students[3] indicates how pervasive this is. Students were asked "Is it all right if a male holds a female down and forces her to engage in intercourse if . . ."

	Answering Yes	
	Female	*Male*
He spent a lot of money on her?	12%	39%
She led him on?	27	54
They have dated a long time?	32	43
She says she is going to have sex with him, then changes her mind?	21	36
She has let him touch her above the waist?	28	39
She is stoned or drunk?	18	39

It is important to recognize and to alert your teenager to the fact that not all coercion is by physical force, and not all coercion is by males. Many an adolescent has been goaded into having intercourse by peer pressure or by such classic lines as "If you loved me, you would go to bed with me." All teenagers should be taught the obvious answer to that line: "If you really cared about me, you wouldn't want to force me into something I'm not ready for."

Some teenagers, particularly girls, will be physically forced into having intercourse. Teenagers should be aware that there are no situations under which it is appropriate for one person to physically force another into having sex. Both boys and girls should recognize that forced sex of any type, not only by a stranger but by a friend, a date, or even a family member, is rape. The fact that the rape was carried out by a date or an acquaintance in no way excuses the crime or lessens the penalties under state laws. Chapter

14 deals with what your teenager needs to know about forced sex and how to avoid it.

Moral Values as a Factor

You don't simply wake up one day and say, "Ah-hah, I think this is the day I'm going to teach my son or daughter about morals." Morality is something you have been teaching your child since the day he or she was born. Children learn values such as respect for others, honesty, and integrity from watching and listening to their parents. If their parents demonstrate these qualities and there is a basic respect for the parent, the teenager is likely to absorb them.

Of course, since children are rarely privy to their parents' sexuality, sexual values must be dealt with separately. This includes feelings about masturbation, the relationship of love and sex, intercourse, pregnancy, abortion, homosexuality, and a myriad of other issues. Remember, it is not necessary to cover all the relevant topics in a single lecture. You can use a television show or a newspaper article about a specific topic as an entrée into the subject and then share your values. Your teenager may disagree with you. Do not try and cram your beliefs down his or her throat. This is likely to create an atmosphere in which your teenager will become oppositional. Simply listen to his or her thoughts without passing judgment and share your own thoughts and feelings, requesting the same courtesy. Do not get into a debate as to who is right and who is wrong. Just listen and be heard.

Using Good Judgment

Any parent with a teenager who drives a car knows that the best you can expect after providing him with as much information as possible is that he has the wisdom to make the appropriate decisions. He is the one that controls the acceleration and the brakes. Once he is behind the wheel, you cannot make the decisions. The wider the foundation of information and experiences he has to base those decisions upon, the more informed his decision will be. Likewise, your teenager is responsible for the decisions he makes about his own sexuality. You can provide some of the facts, information, and guidance that may influence him, but ultimately the decisions are your teenager's to make.

10

CONCEPTION AND CONTRACEPTION

Whether for the purpose of avoiding an unwanted pregnancy, preparing for the day when babies are desired, or just for the sake of understanding the marvels of the human body, the process of conception is important for your teen to understand. Knowledge of the basics of this wondrous biological process provides a good foundation for understanding related topics such as menstruation, contraception, pregnancy, and the other biochemical aspects of sexuality.

Conception

The miraculous process of conception is extremely complex, and it is not necessary for teens to understand every minute detail. The basics are sufficient. If they seem interested, you might consider renting the outstanding videotape *The Miracle of Life*, which is available at many video stores.[1]

First, teens need to know that although intercourse is the usual means by which sperm are carried to the female, it is by no means the only way. Once the male ejaculates, the semen can accidentally come into contact with the opening of the vagina, allowing the sperm to find their way inside. Likewise, the procedure can be done by artificial insemination, with a physician depositing the sperm through mechanical means.

Once inside the vagina, these microscopic sperm propel themselves by the whipping of their tails, up through the cervix, into the uterus, and finally into the fallopian tubes. If the woman has recently released an egg (ovum), and if it is still present in the tubes, one of the millions of sperm may enter the egg and fertilize it. At this point the woman is pregnant. All it takes is one sperm and one egg. Since sperm are capable of living in a woman's body for up to seven days, conception can sometimes occur a week after intercourse.

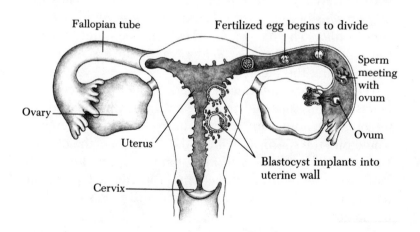

Figure 1. The Uterus and Fertilization

After conception, the fertilized egg begins to divide, first into two cells, then four, eight, sixteen, et cetera. At the same time the egg moves slowly down the fallopian tube toward the uterus. Once at its destination inside the uterus, the egg first attaches itself to, and later becomes buried within, the uterine wall. Slowly, over a period of nine months, the mass of cells separates into different layers and parts of the unborn child's body. For the first eight weeks the developing baby is referred to as an embryo; then, until its birth, as a fetus.

Contraception

The role of contraception for today's teenagers is substantially different from when you were an adolescent. No longer is contraception simply a means of reducing the risk of pregnancy. Nowadays, the use of condoms and contraceptive foam is a *must* for any adolescent who engages in sexual intercourse, *even if the female partner is using another means of birth control such as a diaphragm or birth control pills.* The dangers of AIDS and the other sexually transmitted diseases make condoms and foam essential tools in protecting the life of your child.

Teenagers are notoriously ignorant about birth control. One teenager reported that he and his girlfriend had intercourse standing up, because he had heard that gravity would pull the sperm away from the direction of the uterus. Unfortunately, no one informed him that sperm are excellent swimmers—in all directions. You can get pregnant having intercourse standing on your head. Position does not matter.

I have talked with boys who believed that it is impossible for girls to become pregnant the first time they have intercourse or that withdrawal by the male prior to ejaculation will prevent a pregnancy. Neither, obviously, is true. I've heard teenagers say that to get pregnant, both partners have to reach orgasm, so if one of them refrained from having an orgasm, the girl would not become pregnant. I spoke with one girl who stopped taking birth control pills because they had caused her to gain a few pounds and she was afraid of being fat. She was pregnant.

I've heard of teenagers douching after intercourse with lemon juice, vinegar, commercial douches, and even Pepsi Cola. None of them prevent pregnancy. In fact, the propelling action of the douche may actually push more sperm into the uterus and make pregnancy more likely.

Since there is so much technical information about contraception in this chapter, it should not be presented verbally to your child, but rather in a printed form. In that way he will have more time to digest the information and not feel that it is an assignment to be committed to memory. However, it is essential that he is familiar with the following information—and that you are too, in case your child has questions about it.

Much of the information in this chapter has been taken from *A Young Woman's Guide to Sex* and *A Young Man's Guide to Sex*. A chapter similar to this one can be found in each of those books, geared especially for the male or female teenage reader. However, if you wish, you may reproduce sections of this chapter for your child's use (it is not to be mass reproduced, because of copyright laws).

What Your Teenager Absolutely Has to Know

To deal effectively with contraception, your teenager must at least know four essential things: how condoms are properly used; how they are correctly used in tandem with contraceptive foam; that the responsibility for birth control is his or hers and cannot be delegated to a partner; and most of all that preventing pregnancy has nothing at all to do with luck. It is a matter of knowledge, understanding, and planning.

Teenagers have many excuses when a pregnancy occurs. The following five excuses are the ones that I hear the most when sexual escapades end up in a pregnancy.

Many teenagers fool themselves into believing that *pregnancy is something that happens only to other people.* Approximately three thousand teenage girls will become pregnant *TODAY*, most of them "accidentally." I place the word "accidentally" in quotation marks because this is how most teenagers and parents often view these pregnancies. The reality is that it is not *accidental* at all; it is *irresponsible*. Most of these pregnancies can be avoided if the teenagers have the proper information and if they act in a responsible manner.

Many youths leave the responsibility for contraception to their partner, feeling that their partner is more knowledgeable about birth control or sometimes just assuming that their partner is the one using some form of contraception. The reality is that in a consenting relationship both partners are equally responsible for whatever occurs. Teenagers must be prepared for being sexually active; they must understand how the various contraceptive techniques are used and be ready to implement the method of choice if the need arises. Even if they know that their partner is using the contraceptive method, they must have enough knowledge to be certain that it is being used properly.

Many youths erroneously believe that if they plan for birth control they are going to remove the romance and the spontaneity from the experience, or that contraception will interfere in some way with the sexual experience. The reality is that being prepared can remove much of the worry and anxiety connected with a sexual experience and add to the warmth and enjoyment of the experience. There is nothing loving about taking a risk with a potential unwanted pregnancy.

Most teens are embarrassed to get contraception from a pharmacy or afraid that if they go to a family planning center, their parents might somehow find out. The reality is that just by supplying your teenager with information about contraception, giving him permission to use contraception when the need arises, or giving him condoms, you can vastly reduce this anxiety.

Finally, *many youths worry about the health risks associated with contraceptive methods.* The reality is that there are vastly more medical complications associated with abortion, pregnancy, and childbearing than there are with contraception.

The following section explains the essential facts about the major birth control techniques, both effective and ineffective. Only about 40 percent of teenagers use any method of contraception during their first intercourse, and although the percentage rises with increased sexual experience, only 55 percent of teenagers indicate that they use any contraception regularly.[2]

Contraceptive Methods

"Natural Methods," or Fertility Awareness Methods (Not Recommended for Teenagers)

With natural methods, including the "rhythm method" of birth control, the couple tries to predict when the female is fertile and refrains from intercourse during that time.

Natural methods are placed first in this section not because of their importance as contraceptive techniques, but rather because it is misinformation about these techniques that leads to so many teen pregnancies. *It is recommended that teenagers not use natural methods of birth control, for the following reasons:*

1. Teenage girls tend to be extremely irregular in their periods, and therefore the "right time" is extremely hard to predict. This is true as well for adults, but especially true of adolescent girls.

2. Occasionally, sperm have been found to survive inside a woman's body for up to seven days. Consequently, even if intercourse takes place a number of days before ovulation, it is possible to get pregnant.

3. Teenagers may have good intentions of engaging in intercourse only when it is the "right time," but, unfortunately, in the heat of passion many of them are not able to abstain.

If because of religious reasons, or any other reason, your teenager intends to use one of the natural methods of contraception, he or she should get detailed information on how to implement it from a knowledgeable health care provider at an organization such as Planned Parenthood or from a physician who knows the area. Do not assume that all physicians are informed about natural methods of contraception. Ask before you make an appointment.

The Condom

The purpose of the condom is to act like a bag, collecting the semen and preventing it from entering the vagina. In addition to being a good contraceptive device, condoms protect against sexually transmitted diseases. For this reason, even if your teenager is using another form of birth control, it is essential that the male partner use a condom.

Condoms are sold in a variety of colors and textures, and with or without lubrication. The lubricated ones seem to break less often, and some men report that they feel better. Sold in packs of three or more, each condom is usually wrapped individually in foil. After unwrapping, the rolled-up condom is placed onto the erect penis with one-half inch of room left between the tip of the condom and the tip of the penis to hold the semen after ejaculation. Condoms should *never* be unrolled first and then stretched over the penis. Some condoms come with special reservoir tips, which allow room for the semen to accumulate. The most common mistakes that teenagers make in using condoms are putting them on before going out on a date and attempting to place one on the penis while it is limp. Both these methods will result in failure of the device.

Condoms are usually made of a thin latex or animal membrane and thus do not interfere with the sensations of intercourse. Since latex condoms are thought to be more effective in preventing AIDS than animal membrane condoms, teenagers should always choose latex condoms if both types are available. One note of caution, however, is that latex condoms must never be used in conjunction with an oil-based lubricant such as petroleum jelly (vaseline) or baby oil, either on the penis or in the vagina. The oil will cause the latex to deteriorate and the condom to leak.

Condoms are sold in any drugstore and most supermarkets, often on the open shelves or display stands. No prescription is necessary to purchase condoms. Since teenagers are frequently very uncomfortable with the idea of going into a store and purchasing condoms on their own, it would be helpful for parents to buy some condoms for their teenagers and provide instructions on how they are properly used. Remember, only buy latex condoms and, if the package is dated, make sure they are fairly fresh. Under optimum conditions, condoms are not good for more than one and a half years.

Since the expected failure rate for condoms over a one-year period is about 10 percent, a contraceptive foam containing at least 5 percent nonoxynol-9 should be used along with the condom. This can reduce the failure rate by half and give added protection against both accidental pregnancy and AIDS. The contraceptive foam should be inserted *before* intercourse, but a late application is better than nothing. It is important that the foam never be placed inside the condom, since this will likely cause it to slip off during intercourse. If a condom does slip or leak during intercourse, sperm can enter the vagina, reach the female's egg, and lead to pregnancy. Likewise, a failed condom means semen and vaginal fluids are free to mix, and AIDS or other sexually transmitted diseases are more easily passed.

To prevent the condom from slipping after ejaculation, it should be held securely as the penis is withdrawn from the vagina. This is necessary because the penis usually shrinks after ejaculation and the now loose-fitting condom may slip off, spilling some semen inside the partner. The condom should then be immediately thrown away. Take care not to place the still-wet penis near the vagina. There will still be some sperm on the tip of the penis, and even one drop can cause pregnancy. For this reason, the penis should be washed and dried before the partner is approached. If intercourse is attempted again, a fresh condom and a second application of contraceptive foam must be used.

Vaginal Spermicides: Foams, Jellies, Creams, Suppositories, and Vaginal Contraceptive Film

Contraceptive foams, jellies, creams, and suppositories all work by creating a chemical barrier that kills sperm; therefore they are called spermicides. Foams, contraceptive suppositories, and vaginal contraceptive film can be used as contraceptive methods by themselves, but all three are much more effective when used in conjunction with a condom. Creams and jellies, on the other hand, are designed to be used only with a diapragm or cervical cap.

Contraceptive foam comes in an aerosol can and has a separate plunger-type applicator. Its texture is a lot like shaving cream. The can is first shaken thoroughly (about twenty shakes), and then the applicator is filled. The applicator full of foam is inserted deep into the vagina, and the plunger pushed to disperse the foam.

Foam should be inserted prior to intercourse to kill the sperm. However, because it loses potency over time, it should be inserted no more than thirty to sixty minutes before. If a longer time goes by, more foam should be used. Additional foam must be inserted before *each* act of intercourse. After intercourse it is important to wait at least eight hours before doing anything (like douching) that might wash out the foam. Each package of foam will come with complete instructions. To maximize protection against AIDS, foams with at least 5 percent nonoxynol-9 should be used. Foam also affords some protection against other sexually transmitted diseases and pelvic inflammatory disease (see chapter 12 on sexually transmitted diseases) and can provide a good backup if another method of birth control gets fouled up.

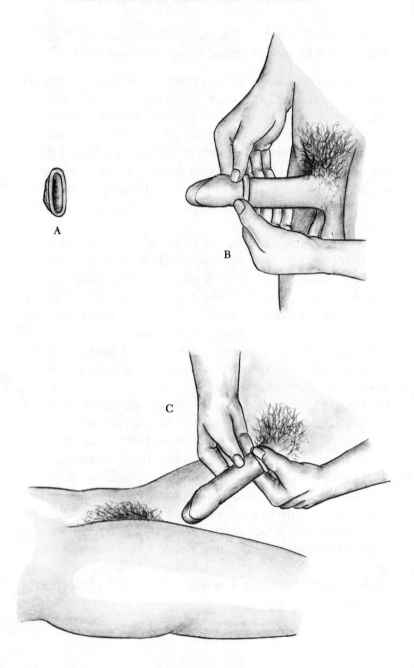

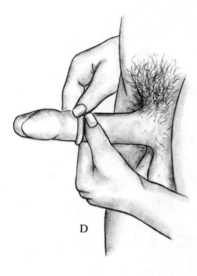

D

Figure 2. How to Use a Condom

(A) Take the rolled condom. (B) Unroll condom onto erect penis, leaving room at the tip for the semen to accumulate. (C) After intercourse, hold condom while withdrawing penis from the vagina. (D) Remove condom from penis while away from partner's vagina. (E) Dry penis and discard used condom before reapproaching partner.

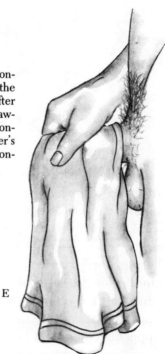

E

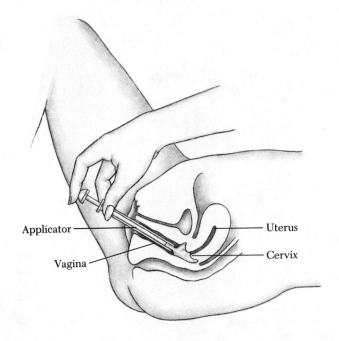

Figure 3. How to Use Contraceptive Foam

Spermicides are also available in suppository form. *Contraceptive suppositories* are wrapped in foil or plastic and contain chemicals similar to those in the contraceptive foams. They do tend to be somewhat less messy than foams and fit more easily into a purse. However, for teenagers, there is one large drawback: it is necessary to wait fifteen minutes for the suppository to dissolve and disperse. Since teenagers are often in a hurry to complete intercourse, suppositories may be somewhat risky. As with foam, a new suppository needs to be inserted before each act of intercourse, and eight hours must elapse before douching the vagina.

Vaginal contraceptive film is another relatively new spermicidal method, which was approved by the FDA in 1986. It is a two-inch-square, paper-thin film containing spermicide that is inserted into the vagina. Insertion should take place no less than five minutes nor more than two hours prior to intercourse. The film dissolves on its own and is washed away by the vagina's natural fluids. A new film needs to be inserted before each act of intercourse.

It is extremely important that teenagers realize there are a vast array of creams, ointments, douches, and other vaginal products on the market that have nothing at all to do with contraception and that will in no way help prevent pregnancy. If they want to purchase a product for birth control, they must be certain that it says "contraceptive" on it.

The Birth Control Pill (Oral Contraceptives)

No doubt the most publicized and the most popular of all birth control methods is the birth control pill (oral contraceptive). The only oral contraceptives currently available in the United States are for women, although some tests have been conducted on pills that men can use. Birth control pills are actually a preparation of synthetic female hormones. There are two main varieties of pills available in the United States, the minipill and the combination pill. Each has its own advantages and disadvantages.

Before your teenager can use the pill as a contraceptive method, she has to have a complete physical examination. Although it is not necessary that a parent attend, it is recommended, since it will also require a thorough discussion of her health history as well as her family's, in order to confirm that she does not have any of the contraindications that make taking the pill dangerous. It will also allow the practitioner to weigh the advantages and disadvantages of each of the types of pills with you and your teenager. Any bothersome side effects should be reported immediately to her physician. Teenagers who take the pill should be seen for a yearly physical and should notify a physician that they are on the pill if any medication is prescribed. This is to eliminate the possibility of unwanted interactions between the medications.

The pill packet will provide instructions that must be followed *exactly*. Teenagers who use the pill should know about and obtain a second method of birth control at the same time, as a backup. This secondary protection must be used during the first cycle of pills, and it can become handy later if your teenager forgets to take some pills, runs out, or decides to stop using the pill. With the minipill it is suggested that the backup method be used during the first several months and even during each midcycle. The backup method should likewise be used if your teenager experiences severe vomiting or diarrhea, since the chemicals may not be getting into the bloodstream in sufficient strength. It is important that the pills be taken consistently and at approximately the same time each day. A teenager who is absentminded or who acts irresponsibly probably should not take the pill.

There can be side effects from birth control pills, although your physician can minimize the possibility of most potentially serious complications by providing a thorough physical examination and taking a complete family medical history. If your teenager experiences any of the following problems after taking birth control pills, see your physician immediately:

- Abdominal pain (severe)
- Chest pain (severe), cough, shortness of breath
- Headaches (severe), dizziness, weakness, numbness

- Eye problems (vision loss or blurring)
- Speech problems
- Severe leg pain (calf or thigh)
- Depression
- Yellow jaundice
- Breast lump

In addition to monitoring for these major side effects, it is important for parents and teens to be vigilant for other changes, such as weight gain or increased irritability. Although these side effects are not potentially as serious as those listed above, they can have dramatic effects on a teenager's self-esteem, and they could influence a teenager to cease taking the pill.

The great advantage of the pill is that it is extremely effective. Theoretically, if used correctly, it should be 100 percent effective. In addition, periods are often shorter, lighter, and less painful. Also, if taken on time, teenagers don't have to remember to carry other contraceptive devices with them or worry that they are being used incorrectly.

The Diaphragm

The diaphragm is a small, dome-shaped, flexible rubber cup that is inserted into the vagina so that it covers the opening of the cervix. It is always used with contraceptive cream or jelly, which is placed inside the dome and around the rim of the diaphragm. Consequently it is effective in two ways: the diaphragm provides a barrier that stops sperm from getting into the uterus, and, if any sperm should slip by, the contraceptive jelly or cream kills them with spermicidal chemicals. If intercourse is repeated, additional spermicide must be inserted each time *but without re-*

moving the diaphragm. The spermicide comes with an applicator that can be used to put it directly into the vagina.

The following are some very important cautions specifically for teenage girls who use the diaphragm:

1. The diaphragm must be fitted by a health care practitioner. Sometimes teenage girls will borrow diaphragms from a friend or even use their mother's. If a teenager intends to use the diaphragm, it should be fitted solely for her.

2. Anyone using the diaphragm should be instructed on its proper use by a health care professional with specific knowledge about this technique. It isn't complicated, but insertion and removal can be tricky the first few times, and some practice is required.

3. Products such as talc, perfumed powders, and petro-

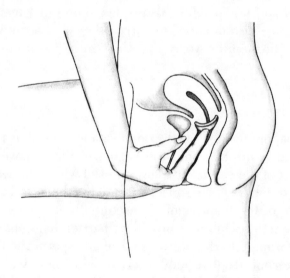

Figure 4. How to Use a Diaphragm

leum jelly (Vaseline) should never be used with the diaphragm, since they will cause it to deteriorate.

4. If a girl loses ten pounds or more, the diaphragm should be refitted. This is especially important since many teenage girls frequently diet.

5. The diaphragm must not be left in place for more than twenty-four hours.

6. Before choosing the diaphragm as the primary means of birth control, a teenager must be honest with herself about how responsible she is. It doesn't work if she goes out while the diaphragm is home in her drawer.

Use of the diaphragm is generally associated with few health risks, and, in fact, it is helpful in reducing rates of sexually transmitted diseases, pelvic inflammatory disease, and cervical cancer. It is an extremely reliable means of birth control when used properly and consistently.

The Cervical Cap

The cervical cap is very similar to the diaphragm in that it is a barrier to the cervix, but it is smaller, thimble-shaped, and fits snugly over the cervix by suction. Unlike the diaphragm, the cervical cap does not require the application of additional jelly after each act of intercourse, and it can be left in place for thirty-six to forty-eight hours. The same cautions that apply to the diaphragm should be heeded for the cervical cap.

The Contraceptive Sponge

One contraceptive technique that is relatively new is the contraceptive sponge. It is a soft, plastic sponge that works similarly to a diaphragm. It is inserted into the vagina and fits over the cervix. However, unlike the diaphragm, the sponge contains its own spermicide and doesn't require the application of creams or jellies. It is disposable, doesn't require a prescription, and is available at pharmacies.

To use it, the sponge is first moistened with water and then inserted into the vagina prior to intercourse, making sure that it covers the cervix. Moistening is essential, not only because it makes insertion easier, but more important because it activates the spermicide. Once inserted, the sponge is checked to make certain that it is sitting against the cervix, with the strap pointed outward toward the opening of the vagina. The sponge should be checked after intercourse to make sure it has remained in place. It must not be removed for at least six to eight hours after intercourse and can be safely left in place for up to twenty-four hours. Repeated intercourse is possible during that time, and, unlike the diaphragm, it is not necessary to apply any additional spermicide. Once removed, it should be thrown away because it is not effective a second time.

There have been some concerns about sponges being related to Toxic Shock Syndrome, a dangerous ailment that occurs primarily in young women. Therefore it is important to follow the instructions carefully. In particular, the sponge should never be left in for more than twenty-four hours and should never be used during menstruation, the first few months after giving birth, or if there is any abnormal discharge from the vagina.

The main advantages of the sponge are its wide availability and easy use. As with other spermicide-plus-barrier methods, it may provide protection against some sexually transmitted diseases and against cervical cancer. Initial research has found its effectiveness comparable to that of the diaphragm for women who have never given birth. Somewhat surprisingly, women who have had children appear

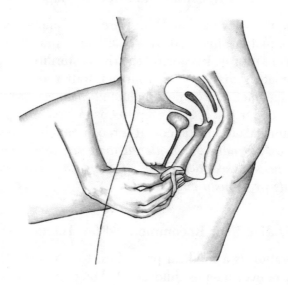

Figure 5. How to Use a Contraceptive Sponge

to have higher failure rates with the sponge than those who have not.

The Morning-After Pill

For girls who have unprotected intercourse, physicians can prescribe what have been called morning-after pills. These are high doses of hormones that, if taken soon after intercourse (within twenty-four to seventy-two hours), appear to be fairly effective. They are most effective when taken within twenty-four hours. Side effects can be quite troublesome, however, and *morning-after pills are not considered to be a safe form of ongoing contraception.*

The IUD (Not Recommended for Teenage Use)

Intrauterine devices, or IUDs, are small metal or plastic devices that are inserted by a health care practitioner into a woman's uterus. Because of the risk of sterility from pelvic inflammatory disease and from perforation of the uterus, many agencies and clinics, including Planned Parenthood, will no longer insert IUDs into teenage girls, except under very unusual circumstances. It is recommended, therefore, that *the IUD not be considered for a teenager unless circumstances prevent the use of any other contraceptive methods previously mentioned.*

Sterilization (Not Recommended for Teenagers)

Sterilization is a medical procedure to eliminate the possibility of ever having children. Although it has become an increasingly popular method of birth control among adults, *sterilization is not recommended for teenagers, except in some medical emergencies, with some genetic conditions, and for those who have already had several children.* The most common form of sterilization in women is the tubal ligation, in men the vasectomy.

Preventing pregnancy is not a matter of luck, but of planning. Teenagers have a large array of birth control methods available to them. The information they receive about these methods should come before their first intimate sexual encounters, not afterward. Making sure your teenager has the proper information about birth control does not *guarantee* that he or she will not be involved in a pregnancy, but it is the best way to increase the odds.

11

THE TRUTH ABOUT AIDS

Without a doubt, AIDS (Acquired Immune Deficiency Syndrome) is the most important sexual issue that your teenager needs to be informed about. At the same time, it is probably the one topic about which he gets the most contradictory and confusing information.

Your teenager's life and the lives of all his sexual partners depend on his having accurate information about AIDS. This is not an overstatement or a scare tactic. It is no longer possible for your teenager to think about the pleasures of sexuality without considering the risks. Unless he understands what it means to be sexually responsible, and unless he realizes that COMPLETELY SAFE SEX IS VIRTUALLY IMPOSSIBLE, he is unprepared to engage in any sexual activity with a partner.

Many people believe that reports in the press about AIDS have been overblown. Nothing can be farther from the truth. If anything, information about AIDS has been reaching the consciousness of the public much too slowly. Here are some key facts that your adolescent *must* know about this deadly disease:

1. *Once the AIDS virus enters a person's body, his fate is sealed. There is no cure for AIDS.* AIDS is a disease that slowly destroys the body's immune system, leaving it vulnerable to many illnesses. Eventually, as the immune system and the body weaken, its victims succumb to any of a number of very unpleasant diseases. AIDS is caused by the Human Immunodeficiency Virus (HIV), and, although initially it was thought that not everyone who contracted the virus ended up with the disease, all current indications are that once the virus enters the body the person will eventually die of the complications of AIDS. Available treatments are designed only to bring temporary relief.

2. *Teenagers are extremely vulnerable to AIDS.* When AIDS first reached public awareness, reports indicated that male homosexuals, intravenous drug users, hemophiliacs, and Haitians were particularly vulnerable to this disease. However, recent information indicates that the disease can be spread through heterosexual intercourse and that anyone who engages in unprotected sex faces the danger of contracting AIDS.

Because teenagers often have a way of minimizing the potential risk of their actions, and because they are sometimes indiscriminate about their sexual partners and careless and/or ignorant about birth control methods, they are especially vulnerable to AIDS. Recent projections indicate that one of the most at-risk groups over the next few years may be teenagers, both male and female, heterosexual and homosexual.

3. *It does not appear that, under ordinary circumstances, AIDS is spread through kissing or casual contact.* However, since saliva and sometimes blood (from gum bleeding) are exchanged in deep kissing (French kissing, wet kissing), scientists have not ruled out the possibility that the virus, *under certain conditions*, might be transmitted in this manner.

AIDS is spread only when the fluids from an infected person are introduced into the body of another person. In infected people, the AIDS virus has been found in virtually every one of their body fluids. However, it is believed that a healthy body can fight off the small amounts of virus found in infected saliva or tears.

4. *The most common way AIDS is spread is through sexual contact.* Your adolescent is at risk if he engages in vaginal intercourse, anal intercourse, oral sex, or any other type of sexual activity in which a bodily fluid is discharged. It is believed that semen is responsible for spreading approximately two-thirds of the cases of AIDS. Withdrawal of the penis before ejaculation is not sufficient to stop the spread of AIDS. The fluids discharged from the penis prior to ejaculation also contain the virus. Anal intercourse is thought to be especially dangerous in the spread of AIDS.

5. *AIDS can also be transmitted through contact with blood or any other infected bodily fluid.* So far this has meant primarily through blood transfusions or the use of contaminated needles to shoot drugs. However, since our focus is on teenage sexuality, these other means of transmission will not be dealt with in any detail.

6. *Teenage girls are at least as vulnerable to AIDS as teenage boys, probably more so.* There seems to be a prevalent attitude that girls are somehow less at risk for AIDS, since most cases have been reported in males. This is not at all true. The reason that males have been more affected until now is because the disease spread first in the male homosexual community and then among intravenous drug users. Now that it has crossed over into the heterosexual community, a greater percentage of women are contracting the disease than in previous years. Because women receive a bodily fluid (semen) from men during sexual activity, it is now thought that females may be at even greater risk than males. At the very least, they are equally vulnerable.

Precautions that Teenagers Must Take

As already mentioned, completely safe sex is virtually impossible. However, there are a number of precautions a teenager can take to greatly reduce his risk of contracting AIDS.

Choosing Whether to Be Sexually Intimate

The first decision your adolescent must make in avoiding AIDS is whether to have sex at all. This consideration used to be based primarily on moral issues. Some teenagers believed that sex was not appropriate until after marriage or at least until after falling in love. Now, however, your son or daughter has an additional consideration. Abstaining from sex can be a health and safety issue, a way in which he can protect himself and possibly even protect his life.

Whatever decision your teenager makes, it is essential that it not be a result of parental pressure. Certainly your input as a parent can be extremely valuable in presenting the pros and cons, but the decision must be his own. Many teenagers will yield to pressure and say whatever is necessary to quiet their parents' fears, then go out and do what they want to do. This is an extremely dangerous way to make what could be a life-and-death decision.

Many teens have good intentions to abstain and then find themselves overwhelmed by passion, with no way of protecting themselves. If your teenager is going to abstain, make it clear to him that he still needs to be aware of the critical role of contraception, not only in avoiding pregnancy, but also in reducing the risk of AIDS. That way, if he gets carried away, at least he will be able to protect himself and his partner.

Choosing a Partner

The only way someone can be absolutely sure of not contracting AIDS from having sex is with a partner who has never been exposed to HIV. Since it is impossible to test every partner (and even if that were possible, the tests are not 100 percent accurate), it is important that your teenager recognize that partners who fall into any of the following categories carry a significant risk of carrying the AIDS virus, and that a choice to have intimate sexual contact may be a life-and-death decision.

- Anyone who has ever tested positive for the AIDS virus (HIV).
- Anyone who is or has been sexually active with other partners (especially prostitutes).
- Any male who has sexual contact with another male.
- Any intravenous drug user.
- Anyone who is bisexual.
- Anyone who received a transfusion of blood or clotting factor between 1978 and 1985.
- Anyone from Haiti or Africa.
- Anyone who suspects that they may have come in contact with the AIDS virus.
- Anyone who has had intimate contact with someone who falls into any of the above categories.

Obviously, teenagers "in heat" are not going to take the time to collect a full case history on their partners. Ideally they should, but realistically they won't. They should at least be aware of the at-risk categories, so that they can screen their potential partners.

Choosing How to Be Sexually Intimate

Certain sexual activities carry greater risk than others. Among the most dangerous are:

- Anal intercourse
- Vaginal intercourse without a condom
- Oral sex
- Any activities involving contact with the anus or rectum

Teenagers should be aware of these high-risk categories so that they can modify their sexual behavior.

Adolescents must also be made aware of the precautions that they must take every time they are going to engage in intercourse or any penetration of another person's body. First, it is essential that the male wears a latex condom, preferably one manufactured with a self-contained contraceptive foam that has at least 5 percent nonoxynol-9, and that he uses it properly. Latex condoms create a barrier so that HIV can neither get in nor get out. Animal membrane condoms are not thought to protect against transmission of the AIDS virus.

Second, just as condoms are not a foolproof means of preventing pregnancy, they are not a perfect means of preventing the spread of AIDS. Early tests indicate that nonoxynol-9, in addition to being an excellent spermicide, may be helpful in killing off any of the AIDS virus that may be present. Consequently, not only should the male use a condom, but the female partner should use a contraceptive foam that contains nonoxynol-9. As with contraception, the combination of condom and foam is much more effective than either method by itself. Foam should not be placed inside the condom, since this will cause it to slip off.

Both teenage boys and teenage girls should understand

how condoms and foam are used properly. If either is used incorrectly, it is worse than using nothing at all because it gives the young couple a false sense of security.

Choosing When to Be Sexually Intimate

The final element of safer sex for your teenager is never making a decision to have sex while using drugs or alcohol. As with driving under the influence, his decision-making process will be seriously impaired, and he will be much more likely to make impulsive, unsafe decisions. If he is going to be sexually intimate, he should make that decision free from the distortions of drugs or alcohol. At least then he will be likely to look more carefully at the alternatives and to take reasonable precautions.

12

SEXUALLY TRANSMITTED DISEASES

When I was growing up, all the guys joked about syphilis, "the syph," as we called it. No one ever thought seriously about really getting it or any other venereal disease (that's what they were referred to as back then; now they're called sexually transmitted diseases, or STDs), but we heard a lot about it. When I reached college, the talk was about "the clap," gonorrhea; then in the seventies it was about "super gon," those penicillin-resistant strains of gonorrhea that returning GI's were bringing home from Vietnam. In the early eighties the big news in sexually transmitted diseases was herpes. Its epidemic proportions made the front covers of leading newsmagazines, and talk of syphilis, gonorrhea, and "super gon" virtually evaporated. Now, with the explosion of information about AIDS, you don't even hear about herpes. It's as if all these diseases have vanished. Unfortunately, they have disappeared only from the headlines and from the consciousness of the American people.

The reality is that these diseases are more dangerous than ever. Not only because their epidemic proportions continue unabated, but also because it is believed that infection with some sexually transmitted diseases may increase the risk of contracting AIDS.

Obviously, as a parent, there is no way you are going to go into a detailed explanation of every sexually transmitted disease with your teenager. Rather than deal with the specifics of each disease separately, what is more important is for you to be able to effectively communicate to your teenager that sexually transmitted diseases are not a joke and are not something that happens to other people. The risks of your adolescent contracting an STD are extremely high. It is critical that your teen understand how vulnerable he is to these diseases, what he can do to avoid them, how he can recognize if he has one, and what to do if he is uncertain.

The following information has been adapted from *A Young Man's Guide to Sex* and from *A Young Woman's Guide to Sex*. Both these books contain considerably more detailed information about STDs, but the following information was chosen because it is the very minimum that your teenager *must* have. As with those two books, this portion is addressed to your teenager, rather than to you, the parent. This approach is adopted because teenagers rarely want to get into discussions with their parents about the intricacies of sexually transmitted diseases; they are much more likely to absorb information about this topic by reading it themselves. Read through the material yourself so that you understand the importance of the issues and the information. Then let your teenager read it.

Transmission of STDs

If you are like most teenagers, getting a sexually transmitted disease (STD) is one of the farthest things from your mind when you think about intimate physical contact. You probably wouldn't be surprised at all if you caught a cold or the flu, but catching an STD may seem beyond imagination. Think about that for a minute. If you can catch a cold or the flu from being close to someone who is ill, why is it strange to think that you could catch an STD from pressing your lips against someone or having your body in intimate contact with another person's genitals? The fact is that the closer the physical contact you have with people, the easier it is to catch certain diseases.

There is nothing mysterious about AIDS, gonorrhea, syphilis, herpes, or other STDs. They are illnesses like a cold or the flu, with some important differences:

1. They are usually transmitted through heavy petting or intimate sexual contact.

2. Unlike a cold or the flu, they do not run their course and then go away. Sexually transmitted diseases should be treated by a physician; otherwise they can do significant damage to your body or eventually kill you, *even if the symptoms disappear.*

And there is one other difference. Because of distorted stereotypes, many people think of STDs as being even worse than the plague. They think that STDs are caught only by "dirty," "bad," "immoral," or "sexually loose" people. Too often the stigma attached to these diseases can lead someone to put off going in for tests or getting the necessary treatment. Embarrassment also sometimes prevents people from informing their sexual partners that they might have a disease, even though this information is essential and can actually save someone from becoming very sick or even sustaining serious physical damage, such as infertility.

STDs are so common in the United States, especially

among teenagers and young adults, that some of them have been declared "pandemic" (this means more widespread than an epidemic). According to the Centers for Disease Control in Atlanta, for every 1,000 teenagers in the United States between the ages of fifteen and nineteen, approximately twelve cases of gonorrhea or syphilis are reported. This number includes merely the reported cases of only *two* STDs. In addition, many cases of gonorrhea and syphilis are left out of these statistics because not everyone seeks treatment. If all actual cases of STDs were included, the rate would certainly be several times higher.

Consequently, if you are a high school student and there are 1,000 students in your school, on the average you might expect that there would be between 100 and 200 cases of sexually transmitted diseases during the four years you attend. Certainly the rate at your school may be higher or lower than the national average, but the point is clear: all sexually active teenagers share a significant risk of getting STDs.

The incidence of STDs in teenagers has gotten out of control for several reasons. The two biggest factors are that more teenagers are sexually active and that they tend to have more partners. A third reason is the decline in the popularity of the condom and spermicides as contraceptive measures, methods that provide some protection against STDs. And, fourth, many people who are without symptoms don't know that they have an STD and unknowingly spread their disease to others.

General Guidelines for Preventing STDs

If you are sexually active, there is no sure-fire way to prevent getting a sexually transmitted disease. These diseases can be spread by sexual intercourse, kissing, touching, or even just close contact. So avoiding intercourse does not completely eliminate the possibility of contracting an STD. There are, however, some procedures that can help reduce the risk.

1. The most effective measure is to limit your possible exposure by not having multiple sex partners or not having sex with someone who has multiple partners. Couples who have sex only with each other have a lower rate of STDs than people who have more casual or varied sexual relationships.

2. Don't engage in intercourse or have any genital contact with any person you know to have an STD or who shows any symptoms of an STD. The more familiar you are with these symptoms (listed in this chapter), the better chance you have of avoiding them.

3. Use condoms whenever engaging in intercourse or any intimate genital contact.

4. Use contraceptive foams, creams, or jellies, containing at least 5 percent nonoxynol-9, since they may reduce your risk of contracting AIDS as well as some other STDs.

5. Urinate and wash your genitals after having intercourse. Urination may flush out bacteria before they begin to travel up the urethra, and washing can cleanse away much of the bacteria.

6. Gargle with saltwater after oral sex. This may help to flush STD germs out of the mouth.

7. Maintain good general health and hygiene. Proper rest, nutrition, stress reduction, exercise, and cleanliness are important in maximizing your resistance to infection.

8. If you are having intercourse with different partners or with someone who may be sexually active with other

partners, have a medical examination for STDs at least twice a year.

Early Symptoms of STDs

As was just mentioned, one of the aspects of STDs that makes them so difficult to eliminate is that a person may have one of these diseases and have no symptoms at all. This is especially true for females, which is an important reason for sexually active women to have regular medical checkups.

When symptoms are present, they can vary widely. Remember, the term STDs does not stand for one disease, but for a group of different diseases. You can even have more than one of them at the same time. Below is a list outlining the most common early symptoms of sexually transmitted diseases in both sexes.

Burning urination—A painful burning sensation when urinating.

Discharge—A white, yellowish, greenish, and/or foul-smelling discharge from the vagina or anus of females, or a clear, yellowish, or milky discharge from the penis or anus of males.

Itching—Itching anywhere in the pubic area, inside the vagina, penis, anus, or in any of the hairy portions of the body.

Night sweats—Heavy sweating in the nighttime, even if the temperature is comfortable.

Pain in the lower abdomen or pelvic area—This can be a sign of an STD that has spread internally.

Rashes—Rashes, particularly in the genital area, chest, on the soles of the feet, or on the palms of the hands.

Sore throat—A sore throat after engaging in oral sex.

Sores—Any sores, especially in the genital area, whether painful or painless.

Warts—Any warts or bumps in the genital or anal area.

What to Do if You Have Any Symptoms of STDs

If you are aware of having any of the early symptoms of STDs, it is important that you get them checked right away. (The appendix gives information on how and where you can get help.) Don't wait to see if the symptom persists, and don't try to treat yourself. Many of the early symptoms of STDs disappear completely or go "underground" after the first few weeks while the disease continues to exist in your body and in fact may be entering a more destructive phase. Even if the initial symptoms have disappeared, don't assume that it was a false alarm or that your body has rid itself of the disease. At the first sign of a possible STD, immediately have yourself checked by a physician. Not being examined can lead to great physical harm to yourself and others. You also need to go to a physician if you have had sex with someone who develops symptoms or is diagnosed as having an STD. It is essential to follow your doctor's instructions for taking medications and to keep all your return appointments: your good health and your ability to eventually have children may be at stake.

Don't quit taking the medicine just because the symptoms have disappeared. If you are dissatisfied with the care given by your physician, get a second opinion. There now exist many agencies that are happy to give sensitive, caring treatment to teenagers for little or no cost.

If you find that you do have a sexually transmitted disease, it is essential that you inform any partners with whom you have had close physical contact. Otherwise they can become seriously ill, spread the disease to others, and even reinfect you. Also avoid sexual contact until your treatment is complete, or if you have herpes, at least until the sores are healed.

If you are diagnosed as having the AIDS virus (HIV positive), seek counseling immediately from an agency that treats AIDS patients. You can call the National AIDS Hotline for a referral (see listing in Appendix, p. 197).

13

HOMOSEXUALITY: THE FEARS AND THE REALITIES

Although the sexual revolution of the sixties and seventies has made it possible for homosexuality "to come out of the closet" and gain a degree of acceptance in the public eye, it continues to be something most parents find difficult to accept in their own children. Homosexuality is acceptable as a way of life only when it is someone else's family that is affected.

Underlying this aversion are two prime components. The overt reason is that parents are afraid of the discrimination and ostracism their children might face in a world oriented toward heterosexuals. However, there is often the unstated fear in parents' minds that a homosexual child is living documentation of their failure as a parent. Perhaps in hopes of anticipating and forestalling this unwanted life-style, many parents search for signs of their child's masculinity or femininity, under the false assumption that this will provide a gauge of homosexual tendencies.

Is it OK for my child to play "doctor" and examine another child's body? Is it OK for my son to dress up in his mother's clothes and put on her makeup or for my little girl to be a tomboy? Until what age? At what age should my adolescent be interested in the opposite sex? With some parents these concerns are fleeting thoughts, but others are deeply worried that their child is homosexual. Almost always these thoughts are private. Rarely, if ever, are they openly voiced, even to a spouse.

Parents have a difficult time evaluating these behaviors for two reasons. First, there are no published standards or tables that tell at what age each of these behaviors is typical and at what age it is a warning of problems to come. Second, many preteens and adolescents are very secretive, or at the very least private, about their sexuality. Often what we see on the surface is only a portion of the total picture. We don't usually have a window through which we can view their subconscious feelings and concerns about their sexual maturation and about their masculinity or femininity. And when we do get a brief glimpse of this, we tend not to know what to make of it.

Adolescent Fears

For the teenager, too, this notion of masculine/feminine is confusing. Most teenagers spend their time trying to look and act like other teens and being afraid to do anything that might make them different. Inside their minds they fight their own uniqueness. They know they are different from their friends, but often they experience that distinctiveness as a threat rather than as the gift that it is. Consequently most teens react to the concept of male/female as if it should be an all-or-nothing thing. You are male and therefore you should act and feel one way, or you are female and should act and feel a different way. Unfortunately, that's not the way it works. Every male and every female is unique. There is no single way that a "real" man acts, nor a single way all women act.

Because of this insecurity, many youths tend to confuse masculinity/femininity with sexual orientation. The boy who does not match the subjective definition of "masculine" or the girl who too closely resembles it is suspected of being homosexual. For fear of arousing anyone's suspicions, teens won't discuss homosexuality openly, only in the form of a joke or a negative remark. Thus teenagers tend to remain extremely ignorant about the realities of homosexuality.

Teenage boys seem especially defensive about their masculinity and are very fearful of anything that might diminish their masculine image. They are constantly comparing themselves. In locker rooms, boys sneak a glance at other boys' penises and, to their horror, discover that theirs don't match up in size. They never discuss this fear but just let it fester inside while they try to prove their masculinity in other ways.

Being masculine, macho, one of the guys, et cetera, is extremely important for the typical male teenager. To be anything less invites potential ridicule and harassment, often in the form of homosexual labels. A boy who is quiet and shy or one who is sensitive, cries, or dresses in an unusual manner is often labeled a "fag," "homo," "queer," or some other derogatory synonym for "homosexual." Although this labeling is often just a form of play for the teens doing the name calling, for the stigmatized youth it can be devastating.

John was a fifteen-year-old boy who [feared] . . . he was a homosexual. Although he in no way felt sexually attracted to other boys, in his own mind John had put together a number of unrealistic fears and a lot of misinformation and reached the conclusion he was "gay." Following is the information that John distorted to reach his erroneous conclusions.

1. Apparently because he was shy and unathletic, boys teased him by calling him "gay," "fag," "homo," or other terms that implied he was a homosexual. Not realizing that many boys do this as a way of teasing, he assumed that they saw something about him that looked "gay," and began to worry that maybe they were right.

2. John worried that he masturbated "too much." Although John had no idea what a "normal" amount of masturbation might be, he was positive that the amount he was masturbating was "too much."

3. John was shy with girls. Even though he felt sexually attracted to them, his fear of socializing with girls made him doubt his masculinity. He was not aware that neither shyness nor masculinity has anything to do with homosexuality.

4. John had been molested as a young child by an adult male, who made John play with the man's penis. John decided that this must be the event that caused his homosexuality. . . .

Although John had other problems that required him to remain in counseling almost a year, his sexual fears . . . were reversed within three months, after he fully understood how his misconceptions about masculinity, sexuality, and homosexuality combined to cause him unnecessary [worries].[1]

Possibly because holding, hugging, and kissing are more acceptable among females than among males, or maybe because young girls tend to talk more openly with one another, they do not seem to be as threatened about homosexuality and gender identity as boys are. For some girls, however, issues like being a "tomboy," being athletic, or even simply having a crush on another female can be extremely confusing.

113

Homosexuality—Understanding and Communicating the Truth

Since homosexuality is a very sensitive subject for most teens as well as for their parents, they tend to avoid discussing it. However, it is a topic that you must deal with. Many teenagers will at one time or another wonder whether they have homosexual tendencies. For most these are just mild concerns that evaporate with increased maturity. For others, however, fears about homosexuality can be consuming.

Probably the best way to approach the topic of homosexuality is to bring it up in relation to some article in the paper or some comment that is made. Since many teenagers loosely toss around terms like "fag," "dyke," and other derogatory slang, their use of such an expression can be a perfect opportunity to see if they know what they are talking about and to discourage them from making negative remarks.

Once the conversation is initiated, it is important to clear up any confusion between the concept of masculinity/femininity and homosexuality. There is virtually no relationship between the two. The absence of stereotyped masculine/feminine interests does not indicate that someone is homosexual, nor does the presence of those interests guarantee that the person is not. Heterosexuals vary in interests, occupations, personality, and in virtually every other way, just as homosexuals do. Homosexuality simply has to do with one's sexual orientation; nothing else! A homosexual is a male or female whose primary sexual interest is in people of the same sex. A heterosexual is a person whose primary sexual interest is in people of the opposite sex.

It should be noted that numerous female homosexuals

prefer to be called lesbians. Many homosexuals of both sexes now prefer the term "gay," because it is associated with feelings of joy and pride, rather than the term "homosexual," which has often been used against them as a label for ridicule.

Let's examine the most common myths about homosexuality and substitute the facts in place of the misconceptions.

Myth 1. You can tell a homosexual by the way he or she acts, dresses, or talks.
Fact 1. The stereotypes of gay men acting or even dressing in very feminine ways and lesbians being very tough and "mannish" are for the most part inaccurate. Most homosexuals do not talk, act, or dress any differently than heterosexuals. Certainly there are some gays who act or dress in a flamboyant manner, but then again, many heterosexuals are equally outstanding in their dress or behavior. Most homosexuals appear indistinguishable from heterosexuals.

Myth 2. Homosexuality is an indication that a person has serious psychological problems.
Fact 2. Most psychologists, psychiatrists, and other mental health professionals now agree that homosexuality is not a mental disorder. Rather, they believe that homosexuals are simply people who have different sexual interests than heterosexuals. Most homosexuals lead a perfectly comfortable life and appear to have no more mental problems than do heterosexuals.

Myth 3. Any person who engages in sexual activity with a partner of the same sex is a homosexual.
Fact 3. It is important to understand that having some homosexual fantasies, or even having some sexual encoun-

ters with a partner of the same sex, does not make a person homosexual. This kind of harmless experimentation is common and normal among children and early adolescents. Unfortunately, fear and a lack of understanding about this very point lead to unnecessary doubt and guilt for countless teenagers.

Larry was eleven when out of curiosity he and a fifteen-year-old boy began to experiment sexually with each other. The experimentation only occurred twice, but Larry carried with him for years both the memories of the physical pleasure and a feeling of extreme guilt . . . that he had done something terribly wrong. . . . Since this had been the one pleasant sexual experience in his life, he would sometimes fantasize about it as a way of "turning himself on" during masturbation. At other times when he masturbated, he fantasized about girls. Unfortunately, although he felt attracted to girls, his attempts to gain their attention always seemed to end with his getting teased or made fun of. . . . As he got older, Larry avoided all sexual contact with both men and women. He felt completely "turned off" by any thought of being sexually involved with a male, but had labeled himself as a "homosexual" because . . . of his sexual fantasies. . . . He did feel some attraction to women, but was fearful that they would discover his "homosexuality."

After entering therapy, it took nearly two years for Larry to undo the damage he had brought upon himself. His lack of understanding about the two brief sexual incidents when he was eleven years old, together with an ignorance about sexuality and homosexuality, resulted in many years of unnecessary doubts about himself.[2]

Myth 4. Homosexuality is an all-or-nothing thing. You are either entirely heterosexual or entirely homosexual.
Fact 4. In the early 1950s, Alfred Kinsey, a famous sex researcher, shocked the public by reporting that 37 percent

of men and 13 percent of women interviewed said that between adolescence and old age they had at least one homosexual encounter to the point of orgasm. Kinsey also reported that only 4 percent of the males and 2 percent of the females surveyed were exclusively homosexual.[3]

Although the percentages from Kinsey's report may or may not be applicable to today's world, the concepts are. There are some people who are exclusively homosexual or heterosexual in their sexual orientation. On the other hand, there are some gays who enjoy heterosexual contacts and some heterosexuals who have occasional homosexual experiences. Homosexuality is not all or nothing.

Myth 5. Homosexuals are not capable of engaging in meaningful relationships.
Fact 5. Just as heterosexuals may establish romantic or emotional attachments, so too do homosexuals. Likewise, there are both heterosexuals and homosexuals who engage in sex without any interest in a meaningful relationship.

In order to diffuse the anxiety that youths and parents have about homosexuality, it is essential to differentiate the facts about homosexuality from the fiction. If after reading this chapter you think that your child has some serious confusion or concerns about his or her sexual preference, or if you have any apprehension about your child's direction or lack of direction regarding sexual preference, Chapter 19, "The Homosexual Teenager," will be helpful.

14

PREVENTING SEXUAL EXPLOITATION

It is unfortunate that so much of this book need be devoted to the topic of protecting your teen from the dangers and the problems of sexuality. Playing the role of protector is an inescapable part of parenthood in the late twentieth century; in fact, parents have played this role throughout time. Just as animals protect their young from the dangers of predators, so our role as human parents is to safeguard our children from predators of a not-so-different type.

The difference, of course, is that animals seem to instinctively know when they and their youngsters are in danger. They recognize their enemies and take protective actions at the first sight of a potential intruder. In protecting your teenager against the dangers of violent society, it is often difficult to tell the wolves from the sheep. As a parent, all you can really do is to teach your adolescent the skills to protect him or herself from potential danger, and hope that the time never comes when she or he needs to use them.

In reading this chapter, you will find that much of the information is geared to young women and their parents. That is because females are the victims of sexual crimes in far greater numbers than males. However, it should be emphasized that this is *not* a chapter for parents of girls only. Boys too are sometimes the victims of rape and molestation. Besides, the information in this chapter can be just as important in helping to prevent your son from perpetrating a sexual assault.

If your teenager has been or becomes the victim of a sexual assault, there is a separate section in chapter 17 designed to help you and your teenager through the trauma.

Teaching Sexual Responsibility and Self-Protection

Obviously, the first step in helping a teenager become informed about self-protection is to get him or her to understand the risk. This is not as easy as it sounds. Most teenagers will resist sitting down and discussing how to protect themselves when they don't perceive that there is the slightest bit of danger. That is human nature. Most of us prepare for disasters only after one has already occurred. Most likely you'll get some sort of comment like: "You're always such an alarmist. Don't worry, I can take care of myself." Don't give up.

At a time that seems appropriate, make an attempt to sit down and discuss sexual exploitation with your teenager. Unlike with STDs and contraception, this information takes less technical expertise on the part of the parent.

Before going into the dangers of being subjected to forced sex or acquaintance rape, it is important that teenagers, male and female, understand that sex is a loving act and therefore requires two consenting persons. Both partners in a sexual encounter have the responsibility to set their own limits and to be responsive and accepting of their partner's limits. It should be made clear to boys that when a partner says "no," it means no. To do otherwise is both to break the trust of the relationship and to risk breaking the law and being sent to jail. To act on the old myth that when a woman says "no" to sex she really wants to be taken forcefully is to make a dangerous assumption. Likewise, girls should be made aware that many boys believe this old wives' tale and that some boys may be very persistent. All teenagers should be advised to give a clear and firm message in setting their limits, and not to let themselves get talked or bullied into a situation that they don't want. Sexual freedom includes the freedom to say "no."

If you can get an open discussion going, that's terrific. Don't expect it, however. This information does not lend itself readily to open discussion. If you get too much resistance, simply let your teenager know that forced sex is never appropriate, and that you have some information that might be helpful. Hand over a copy of the following pages and encourage discussion. Follow up at an appropriate time a few days later by asking if the material has been read. If it has been, ask for reactions about a few key points, just as a way of drawing your teenager into a discussion. If your child hasn't read the material, assign a date by which you want it read. Again, don't be afraid to follow up.

The remainder of this chapter is written to your teenager. Read the information for your own knowledge, so that you can be more conversant about it if your teen is willing to discuss some of the material or has some questions.

Understanding the Reality of the Danger

It is important for you to understand that sexual exploitation is not something that happens only to other people. Rape is the most frequently committed violent crime in the United States today. In a study by Robert Coles and Geoffrey Stokes, 14 percent of the teenage girls surveyed indicated that they had been raped. And, according to this survey, the myth that rape is perpetrated by strangers is *absolutely false. The much greater danger is from friends, relatives, and acquaintances.* When asked to identify the rapist, the girls indicated the following:[1]

Identity of Rapist	Percentage
Boyfriend	16%
Friend	30
Neighbor	9
Relative	13
Stranger	29
Gang Rape	4

Other surveys have indicated that as many as 50 to 80 percent of women have experienced some form of sexual coercion.[2]

Acquaintance Rape

It is extremely important that all teenagers, male and female, recognize that to force anyone into unwanted sexual activity is rape. Some boys coerce a girl into having sex by physical force, threats, or intimidation, not realizing that they are committing a serious crime. Many girls do not report these assaults because they are embarrassed, afraid of getting their friend into trouble, afraid they will be blamed, or for various other reasons.

The results of acquaintance rape are no less devastating than if the rape was carried out by a stranger. As a matter

of fact, girls who are the victims of forced sex by an acquaintance may have more emotional scarring than those
raped by strangers, probably because they are more likely
to feel guilt, shame, or personal responsibility for the incident. Because of this they tend to hold in their feelings
and may not seek emotional support. In addition, every
time they see their attacker or hear his name they are
continually reminded of the incident.

The fact is that *forced sex is illegal, even if the person is
a friend, a relative, or a date.* Let a parent or some other
trusted adult know if someone even attempts any type of
sexual coercion.

The purpose of this chapter is not to prevent you from
enjoying dating. It is to alert you to the fact that many
adolescent girls eventually face situations in which a partner
will try to impose his sexual desires. The following paragraphs give a number of suggestions that can help you avoid
or deal with such an eventuality. These suggestions are
broken into three categories: suggestions for lessening the
risk of forced sex and for dealing with an attack (reprinted
from *A Young Woman's Guide to Sex*), suggestions for security, and suggestions for responding to an attack (both
reprinted from the *Sexual Assault Prevention Handbook*,
published by the California Attorney General's Office,
Crime Prevention Center, 1982).

Suggestions for Lessening the Risk of a Forced Sexual Attack Occurring and for Dealing with an Attack

1. If you feel uncomfortable about going somewhere or
being alone with someone, don't go.

2. Be careful of someone who invades your personal space by doing things such as standing or sitting too close, staring at your breasts or crotch, or touching you more than you want. Tell him clearly that you want him to stop what he is doing.

3. Be careful of someone who is too domineering and selfish; who tries to get what he wants even at your expense. You may notice that this kind of person ignores your opinions and wishes or reacts angrily when you don't do what he wants. You may also notice that he lacks sensitivity to other people's feelings and is more concerned with his own gratification.

4. Be careful of someone who participates in delinquent activities, hangs out with a tough crowd, or who gets in trouble with the police. Some of these boys may be pressured by peers to prove themselves or may disregard the consequences of their actions. This caution doesn't mean that all boys who rape are obvious delinquents or that all delinquents are rapists. In fact, some rapes have been committed by boys who were popular at school and who were star athletes.

5. Be careful at parties with alcohol and drugs. Some boys will interpret your mere presence there as an indication that you want sex. Alcohol and drugs can lower a boy's restraints and at the same time make it hard for you to use good judgment. In fact, group or gang rapes, where several boys rape one girl, are more likely to happen in such settings.

6. Don't accept a ride home or go somewhere alone with someone you've just met.

7. Always have a backup to get a ride home or a way out of a risky situation. Arrange with your parents or friends to be able to call them if you need your own transportation.

8. Be aware that boys may misinterpret your dress or

behavior and be prepared to clarify what you do and do not want.

9. Be prepared to deal with pressure to have sex if you date a boy with a reputation for being fast.

10. If you get in a situation in which you are being coerced, pressured, threatened, or forced, *respond quickly and firmly.* Research on attempted but successfully averted date rapes found that the females used three strategies: *fleeing or trying to flee; fighting back; and yelling.* This makes it clear that you are not playing hard to get and at the same time alerts anyone in the area that you need help.[3]

Suggestions for Security

Outside Security

- Stay in a well-lighted area as much as possible.
- Walk confidently and at a steady pace. A rapist looks for someone who appears vulnerable.
- Walk on the side of the street facing traffic.
- Walk close to the curb. Avoid doorways, bushes, and alleys where a rapist can hide.
- If you think you are being followed, walk quickly to areas where there are lights and people. If a car appears to be following you, turn and walk in the opposite direction.
- Be careful when people in cars ask you for directions. Always reply from a distance and never get close to the car.
- If you believe you are in danger, don't be reluctant to scream and run. Consider carrying a whistle or any type of noisemaker. And, if you're in trouble, use it!

- If you are in trouble, attract help in any way you can. Scream, yell for help, yell "Fire!" or break a window. Remember, if a weapon is involved, your choices will be limited.
- Probably the most effective deterrent to any type of attack is to travel with a friend whenever possible.

Home Security

- Make sure all doors and door frames are solid and sturdy. Entry doors should be solid-core wood or metal. Good locks, such as deadbolt locks with one-inch throws, are a must. Don't rely on chain locks.
- Have your locks changed or rekeyed or a new lock added when you move into a new house or apartment.
- Install a peephole viewer in your door. And use it! Never open your door without knowing who is on the other side.
- Install good exterior lighting around your house.
- Make sure all windows can be locked securely.
- Secure sliding glass doors.
- Be sure to use these door and window locks at all times— when you are out and especially when you are home.
- If you live alone (or without a man in the house), do not advertise it. Use only your initials and last name on your mailbox and telephone listing.
- Always check identification before opening your door. Ask that identification cards of repair or salespeople be slipped under your door for you to check. If there is any question, call the person's office. Any reputable sales agent or repairperson will be glad to have you check.
- If strangers ask to use your telephone in an emergency, offer to make the call yourself. Have them wait outside while you make the call.

- If strangers or repairpersons telephone or come to your door, do not admit that you are alone.
- If you live in an apartment, avoid being in the laundry room or garage by yourself, especially at night. Tell your landlord if security improvements are needed. Better lighting, stronger locks, and night security guards are methods to make a building safer.
- If you come home and find a door or window open or signs of forced entry, do not go inside. Go to the nearest telephone and call the police.

Vehicle Security

- After entering or leaving your car, always lock the door.
- Check the backseat before you get in.
- Keep doors and windows closed and locked while you drive.
- If you think you are being followed, drive to a public place or a police station.
- If your car breaks down, open the hood and attach a white cloth to the car antenna. Then wait inside the car with the doors locked. If someone stops to help, stay in your locked car and ask them to call the police or a garage.

Additional Suggestions

The Rape Awareness and Prevention Program at the University of California at Irvine makes these additional security suggestions:

- In elevators, don't get on or off with someone against your instincts.
- Keep emergency phone numbers handy and money to call.

- Don't hitchhike or pick up hitchhikers.
- Hold your keys between your fingers, ready to unlock your car or home.
- Put emergency numbers by the phone.
- Don't stop for a disabled motorist: Call the police from a phone for them instead.
- If someone signals that something is wrong with your car, drive to the nearest station and check.
- Park in well-lighted areas and away from vans or cars with someone "waiting" in them.

Suggestions for Responding to an Attack

Submitting to an Attack

In every rape, the attacker threatens the victim's safety or life. Sometimes a rapist threatens the victim's children or other family members.

If you believe you might get hurt by defending yourself, or if you're afraid to fight back, don't. It is not necessary that you resist. Submitting to a rape out of fear for your own or your family's safety does not mean that you consented. It is still a rape and still a crime, even if you do not have a single cut or bruise. It should be reported to the police. Victims who do not resist should never feel guilty. It is the rapist who committed the crime!

Passive Resistance

Sometimes a victim may want to resist but is afraid to scream or fight back. In these cases, a more passive type of resistance may help to "defuse" the violence of the attacker. With passive resistance you can:

- Try to calm the attacker. Talk to him and try to persuade him not to carry out the attack. If you win his confidence you may be able to escape.
- Claim to be sick or pregnant. Tell him you have VD. This may deter the attacker.
- Try to discourage the rapist. Some women pretend to faint, some cry hysterically, others act insane or mentally incapacitated.
- If you're at home, tell the attacker a boyfriend is coming over or that your husband or roommate will be home soon.

Active Resistance

Nobody can tell you whether active resistance—screaming, struggling, fighting back—will be the "right" thing to do. In some cases, it can frighten off or discourage the attacker. But resistance may also lead the rapist to become more violent or increase his desire to subdue the victim.

There are many kinds of active resistance. Here are some pros and cons regarding the most common ones:

Martial arts—Special self-defense courses, such as judo or karate, are very popular in some areas. Many women have taken courses to protect themselves from attack. If you are proficient in these techniques, they can be very effective. But proficiency takes continuous practice.

Screaming—A scream can surprise or frighten an attacker away if he fears that people will come to help; but screaming won't help in isolated areas.

Struggling and fighting back—A forceful struggle also may discourage the rapist. If you are not afraid to hurt someone, and can land a strong kick or blow, fighting back may give you the opportunity to escape. All blows or kicks must be forceful and should be aimed at vulnerable areas.

Weapons—Some women carry weapons, such as guns, knives, or chemical sprays, to ward off attackers. Unless you are trained and not afraid to use these weapons, they can be very dangerous. The attacker might be able to turn them against you. In the state of California it is illegal to carry some weapons, including all concealed firearms. To legally carry most chemical sprays, you must complete a training course offered by a certified agency or organization. *Check with your local law enforcement authorities before you select a weapon.*

In many cities and towns, groups like the police and sheriff's departments' crime-prevention units, YMCAs and YWCAs, women's clubs, rape crises centers, and local high schools have programs on rape defense and protection. Check with your local groups to see if they offer such help.[4]

III

SPECIAL SITUATIONS, SPECIAL NEEDS

15

THE SEXUALLY ACTIVE TEENAGER

It is really hard to define what exactly a "sexually active teenager" is. All adolescents are sexually active, if not in actual behavior then through their thoughts. In that sense this chapter is certainly applicable for all parents who wish to exert an influence over their adolescent's sexual behavior. However, it is written primarily for those parents who feel that their teenager has prematurely begun to be sexually active or has become "too involved" sexually.

Influence, Yes; Control, No

How sexual should a teenager be? At what age is a certain type of sexual behavior appropriate? Unfortunately, there are no rules to go by. All of us fear for our children and want to help them avoid getting into "hot water." This chapter contains four suggestions that will help you maximize your influence with your adolescent and his sexual behavior.

Suggestion 1. Accept the fact that you are absolutely powerless to *control* your teenager's sexuality. This is not to say that you cannot *influence* his sexual activity, only that you *cannot control it.*

If your teenager and his partner make the decision to be sexually active, they will find a way. It takes only a few minutes to have intercourse; it can be done in the daytime or the evening, in the backseat of a car or in a friend's home. Confining teenagers to the house is not the answer, because eventually they must leave to go to school, work, or a friend's home. Prohibiting them from having sex doesn't work, because they are likely to become more rebellious and show their parents that they can do what they want. Moralizing and guilt are ineffective, because they set up a pattern in which teenagers, even if they abstain through the teen years, are likely to carry over their fears and discomfort about sex into adulthood. *There is no form of physical, verbal, or emotional control that works effectively.*

Take note that suggestion 2, which follows, should not be read in isolation but in conjunction with the rest of the chapter. I say this because I know that many parents are going to have the initial reaction, "This is some more of that bull——, psychological mumbo jumbo, blaming everything on the parents." *That is NOT what suggestion 2 is about.* But you do have to read on to find out what I mean. Don't close the book in anger. If you do, you will only be confirming the point I am trying to get across.

Suggestion 2. As a parent, you must accept some responsibility for the lack of communication between you and your teenager. If you really wish to change what your child is doing sexually, you must stop looking at your adolescent as if he is absolutely wrong and at fault and thinking that if he would just listen to you, everything would be better.

I am not trying to blame your teenager's sexual activity on you. It is his behavior, and he must take responsibility for it. However, as you will find out later in this chapter, the way you communicate with your adolescent may have a significant influence on how open or closed he is to your suggestions and ideas. If you cannot accept that, none of what follows can be carried out effectively.

Let's face it, on our best days we are confused about what our teenagers are all about. Our parents never understood what was going on in our heads when we were teenagers (thank goodness), and we can't know what is going on inside our teen's. As with any human being, there are only two ways to even come close to understanding what teenagers are thinking: by asking them or by having them volunteer the information.

Most teenagers are not going to volunteer information, even when you specifically ask them. Think about that for a second. Why is it your teenager doesn't want you to know what is going on? He is afraid that if you know what he is thinking, you will judge him, disapprove, or in some way try to control his actions. In Coles and Stokes's survey, among teenagers who had engaged in intercourse, 32 percent indicated that their parents definitely knew, whereas 36 percent responded that their parents definitely did not know. The remaining one-third were unsure.[1] If your children are going to talk to you, they first need to trust you.

Trust is not an easy thing to establish with teenagers. As parents, we set rules and standards for them at a time when *they* think they are perfectly capable of making their own decisions. Unfortunately, they often come to look at us as "the enemy," or at least as an adversary rather than an ally. If you wish to establish trust with your teenager, and that is a prerequisite for finding out what is going on in his head, you will first have to recognize that this is a long-term project. As with any "enemy," willingness to "sign a truce" or promise to change behavior will be met with suspicion and mistrust (by both parties).

Suggestion 3 is a real challenge for most parents, but a wonderfully rewarding one if you can carry it off. Likewise, it can help you in your relationship with your spouse and others you may wish to establish relationships with.

Suggestion 3. To establish trust, learn to listen and not judge. When you are listening to your teenager, do not devalue his or her point of view. Be careful. Do not enter any discussion with the unshakable idea that your teenager is crazy or too young to know what he is talking about. If you continually put down his ability to think for himself, it will diminish his self-esteem. Think how it might feel if your boss or your spouse were to indicate continually that you did not know what you were talking about.

Let your teenager know that even if you don't agree, you are willing to accept that he has a right to his own perspective. One caution: once you let him know that you are going to make an attempt to listen more closely, he will test you. It may take a week or a month, but he will test to see whether you are willing to listen openly or whether you will be judgmental and repressive. You have to be very careful not to jump all over him the first time he takes a risk and shares something with you. If you fail the first test, you may not get a second chance. If you pass, more tests will follow.

Suggestion 4 is an extension of suggestion 3, but equally important.

Suggestion 4. If you wish to present your point of view, make sure it is clear that it is *your* point of view, and not *the one and only correct point of view.* Naturally, we think our point of view is the correct one. If we didn't think so, we would change it. However, it is essential in this world that we accept that other people can hold a different point of view and not be wrong. You may strongly disagree with your teenager; if so, tell him your opinion frankly. However, you must accept his right to maintain his own perspective, even if in your opinion it doesn't make any sense.

Setting Rules

Many parents, sensing that they are out of control when it comes to their teenager's behavior, have a tendency to set increasingly stricter rules. Certainly rules have their place in any household, but truthfully, I do not know of a single rule that applies to a teenager's sexual behavior that I believe works successfully. Before you set yourself up in the position of District Attorney, prosecuting every infraction, try to follow the preceding suggestions 1 through 4. The more rules you set, the more controlled your teenager will feel, and the more rebellious he will act. If you do set rules, do so only under the following three conditions. After you read these three criteria, I think you will understand why rules about sexual behavior do not work.

1. Never set a rule for your child that will cut him off from talking to you. The following case history exemplifies the potential consequences.

Donna was sixteen when her sister became pregnant. Her parents exploded with rage when they found out. Her father walked out and got drunk the way he usually did under pressure, then came back and nearly destroyed the house. Her mother wept uncontrollably for a week. Finally, not believing in abortion, her sister decided to have the baby. In the heat of all this, her father said very clearly to Donna: "If you ever let this happen to you, you'll never step foot in my house again." Consequently, when Donna became pregnant two years later, she decided that there was no way her parents would find out. Fearing abortion and equally fearing her parents, Donna put off her decision, first for one month, then two, and then three. Twenty-two weeks into her pregnancy she decided to get an abortion, but now was having trouble finding a doctor who would do it. Finally, because her pregnancy was beginning to show, and because of the severe emotional pressure, Donna attempted suicide. Since her father's threat had made it impossible for her to reach out to her parents for help, Donna very nearly succeeded in killing herself.

2. Don't set rules about things you can't monitor. For example, do not tell your child that you absolutely forbid them from having intercourse or masturbating. You cannot monitor these. You can certainly tell them that you don't approve of these behaviors, if that is how you feel. If your teenager trusts your judgment, he will listen to your concerns and fears. You will not need to set a rule. If your adolescent is rebellious or oppositional, to tell him that he can't do something is like waving a red flag in front of him.

3. If you do set a rule, you must be willing to impose consequences that fit the offending behavior and to implement the consequences if the rule is broken. How many times have you heard a parent say "If you ——, I'll break your neck!" or "If you do that one more time, you won't be let out of your room for a year!" Now, I realize that as parents we sometimes lose our cool and say stupid things. I've done it, you've done it, we have all done it. However, if you set up rules where the consequences are absurd, your teenager will likely ignore you.

Other Considerations with the Sexually Active Teen

Obviously, if your teenager is going to be sexually active to the extent of having intercourse, or even approaching intercourse, it is vital that he or she have very specific information about sexually transmitted diseases and contraception, as well as general information about sex. In addition to any verbal instruction you may give your teen, it is vital to supply written information that can be consulted whenever the need arises.

You have got to ask what kind of birth control method the young couple is using, and strongly suggest the use of condoms and foam in addition to any methods they may presently have. Let the adolescent know about the nearest family planning clinic and suggest that he go there or to your physician for more information about contraceptive methods.

Whatever you do, do not condemn your teenager and make him feel that he cannot come to you in an emergency. Communicate your concerns and fears, but do not put them in the form of prohibitions. Make sure he knows that the door is always open if help is needed.

It should be obvious that there is no way you can protect the sexually active teenager from himself. You can give him the information he must have, let him know what tools he may need, and leave the door open for him to use you as an adviser. However, the final decisions will be his, along with the subsequent rewards and consequences.

16

PREGNANCY

As parents, we all hope our teenagers are smart enough and careful enough to avoid an unwanted pregnancy. However, no matter what steps you take—even if you follow every single recommendation in this book—you cannot control whether your daughter becomes pregnant or your son impregnates his girlfriend. The chances of this happening are greater than you might think. The statistics on teenage pregnancy are staggering. More than one million teenage girls will become pregnant this year. Since each pregnancy requires two participants, that means more than two million teenagers will be involved in pregnancies this year. Add to that the number of teenagers who think that they may be pregnant but are not, and the relevancy of this chapter to all parents of teenagers becomes even more apparent.

Living with the Trauma

The first thing you need to recognize is that you are dealing with an intense emotional crisis. For a teenager to be involved in a pregnancy, or even to go through a false alarm, can be traumatic. In fact, this will probably be a very tense time for your entire family. Even children in the family who are unaware of the pregnancy will likely sense the added tension.

Let your teenager know that you understand his or her anxiety and give him permission to be upset. Share your own concerns and fears, but let your teenager know clearly that you are available to lend support.

Confirming a Pregnancy

Certainly the first step in dealing with a teenage girl who believes she is pregnant is to determine whether that is the case. Since young women often experience irregular menstrual cycles, a missed period does not necessarily mean a pregnancy exists. Even in teenage girls whose periods are fairly regular, fear of pregnancy, severe dieting, or any other type of physical or emotional trauma can cause aberrations in the menstrual cycle.

If a girl's period is even a couple of weeks late, a laboratory test should be done to determine whether she is pregnant. *This is the only way to be certain.* The results of the test will relieve her anxiety if she is not pregnant or allow her to move into the next phase of decision making if she is.

Laboratory tests are available from your regular physician or through an agency such as Planned Parenthood (listed in the appendix). Although do-it-yourself pregnancy tests available at pharmacies are fairly reliable if used as directed, they are not recommended for teenagers unless used under the supervision of a parent. This is because teenagers frequently vary the directions, either out of fear that a parent might find the test or for other reasons. This may invalidate the results. Any conclusions derived from a home test should always be confirmed by a follow-up laboratory test.

Making Decisions about the Pregnancy

If pregnancy is confirmed, your teenager will experience a period of intense emotions. Some teenagers express these emotions openly, whereas others try to hide them, but for almost all of them you can bet that this is an extremely difficult time.

Your teenager will have to make some incredibly important decisions in a period of just weeks or months. Try to be a part of that decision-making process. Do not, however, take the responsibility for making the decisions, unless you feel that your teenager is truly incompetent to do so. Below are a list of the major decisions your teenager will have to face.

Young Man's Decision. What is the best way to help my partner? The first thing your son needs to do is to become involved in the decision-making process. If he avoids participating and instead dumps all responsibility onto the girl, he is putting himself in the position of letting someone else make decisions that will critically affect the remainder of his life.

Ultimately, it is the pregnant girl who has the power to decide the fate of the fetus growing in her body. Your son, however, can help her make the monumental decision whether she should carry the pregnancy to term (as opposed to having an abortion) and, if so, whether she should keep the baby. And being interested enough to want to be part of the decision-making process is a way to demonstrate support and make a difficult situation a little bit less painful.

This is also a time when your son must determine how important his relationship with the young woman is. If he abandons her now, there is a good chance that her anger and hurt will make it impossible to renew the relationship. *Talk to your son about the alternatives, and encourage him to become part of the decision-making process.* He will be helping his partner and, just as important, he will be accepting responsibility for his actions.

Young Woman's Decision. *Whom can I trust to help me with this monumental choice?* If your daughter is pregnant the decision she has in front of her is indeed a monumental one. And it is a decision only she can make. Try to encourage her to get as much information and input as possible. Support and information from you, from counselors and friends, and from her partner are all essential. The more facts she has, the more informed her final decision will be. Let her know, however, that if any one of these resources turns into a source of pressure, she needs to abandon it. If the teenager makes her decision based upon outside pressures, or if she feels that the decision has been taken out of her hands, then there is considerably more chance that she will feel resentment, possibly for many years. You are probably the most important source of information and support for your teenager. But as difficult as it may be, *you must leave the final decision up to her.* Don't be afraid to voice your opinion; you are, as you have always been, the first model for your child's values and priorities. But you must be clear that the final decision will be hers.

Family's Decision. *Do we need to go for counseling?* Your family has nothing to lose by going for counseling. Pregnancy counseling can provide a clearer understanding of the alternatives that are available by supplying facts and figures, and it may help all family members work through the emotional problems. Some of the agencies listed in the appendix (such as Planned Parenthood) can provide such counseling or refer your family to a qualified counselor.

Young Couple's Decision. What do we do about the pregnancy? This, of course, is the heart of the matter, and it is a very complicated decision. There are three alternatives to consider. One is to end the pregnancy, in other words to have an abortion. The second is to continue the pregnancy and to be involved in the raising of the child. In this case marriage is often a consideration. The third alternative is to continue the pregnancy and to choose not to raise the child. In this case it must be decided whether the baby should be given up for adoption or foster care.

Considering an Abortion

Abortion often seems like the "easiest" solution, especially to teenage boys. After all, as far as many boys are concerned, the girl checks in to the clinic or hospital, goes through a brief medical procedure, and the problem is over with. At least, that is what they often believe.

But that is not a realistic assessment of the process of abortion; certainly not from the girl's point of view. For most girls it is very scary to even think about going through an abortion. They may have fears about dying or fears of never again being able to have children. They may be anxious and uncertain about the procedure. They may have religious convictions that forbid it or they may simply be surrounded by people who do and impose feelings of guilt upon them. Most boys do not experience abortion as deeply.

When performed by a trained professional, an abortion

in the first three months of pregnancy is usually a very safe medical procedure. During these early months the most common form of abortion is the vacuum-aspiration method, in which a small tube is inserted through the cervix to pump out the inside of the uterus. The actual medical procedure takes only a few minutes, although the whole process generally takes from three to four hours when admission, counseling, medical testing, and waiting in the recovery room are included.

A second method, used primarily during the fourth or fifth month of pregnancy, is referred to as a D and E (dilation and evacuation). In this procedure a larger suction tube and other instruments are needed to completely remove the contents of the uterus. General anesthesia and hospitalization are sometimes required for this type of abortion. A similar method, called a D and C (dilation and curettage), is less frequently used during these middle months. In this procedure a small spoon is inserted and is used to scrape the walls of the uterus.

During the later stages of pregnancy, neither the aspiration method, the D and E, nor the D and C can be used. Instead, chemicals are injected into the uterus. The chemicals kill the fetus, which is then ejected from the body within about twenty-four hours in a process similar to labor and delivery. This method of abortion can be very painful, physically and emotionally, and can require that the young woman be hospitalized for two or three days.

Although your teen does not need your permission to have an abortion, many physicians require parental consent after the third month of pregnancy. Abortions are legal throughout the United States up to the twenty-fourth week of pregnancy (although often it is difficult to find a doctor willing to do this procedure after twenty weeks). Individual states have the right to outlaw abortions after the twenty-fourth week, unless the mother's life is endangered by the pregnancy.

Although women usually heal quickly from the medical aspects of an abortion, they and their partners often feel the emotional scars for considerably longer. Before, during, and after, most young women and many young men need considerable emotional support from parents, friends, and from their partners. Be sensitive to that need, even if it is not expressed verbally.

If an abortion is the agreed-upon solution, contact a qualified physician or call a qualified agency such as Planned Parenthood for a referral.

Becoming a Parent

When faced with an unplanned pregnancy, the second alternative that many teenagers consider, either as couples or as individuals, is having the child and becoming a parent. Having a child can certainly be a wonderful experience for the couple who is prepared for it. However, for an adolescent unprepared for the responsibilities of parenthood, a child can seem like a terrible burden. Although children can be a lot of fun to play with or babysit for, becoming a parent involves much more than playing games and babysitting. When the playing and the fun are over, your teenager will be staring into the face of some overwhelming responsibilities. Often, because the new parents are so overwhelmed, many of these responsibilities get shifted onto the infant's grandparents.

It should be decided before the birth how much of the responsibility for raising the child and supporting the child—custodially, financially, and emotionally—each parent and each grandparent will bear. Be very clear in letting your teenager know what role you are willing to play and where you set your limits. If you are silent, your teenager may imagine that you want a much larger or different role than you are truly willing to play. If this discussion is postponed until after the birth, the baby can end up being treated like a football, and the atmosphere between parents and grandparents can become very tense.

Before your teenager firmly decides to become a parent, ask him or her to write down the answers to the following questions. Afterward, sit down and discuss the answers together. This will help your teenager make a more realistic decision.

1. Can I earn enough to support the child?
2. How much time will I have to devote to work to support the child?
3. How much time will this leave me to give the child the amount of love and attention he or she will need?
4. How much time will I need to give my partner in order to maintain the relationship?
5. How much time does that leave me to pursue other plans for my future (school, career, personal)?
6. What plans for the future will I have to postpone or eliminate?
7. How much time will I have to enjoy life?
8. Can I be the kind of parent I would like to be?
9. How much financial, emotional, and other support will my family give me in raising the child?

If the young woman does decide to carry the child to term, good prenatal care will be essential. It is highly recommended that your son or daughter take classes on parenting skills. Again, an organization such as Planned Parenthood may be able to help you fill these needs.

Getting Married

If your teenager makes the decision to raise the child, a separate consideration will be whether to get married. It is important not to let your teenager rush into marriage without first considering the added responsibilities that it entails. Teenagers often naively believe that love is enough to make a marriage work. The Sex Information and Education Council of the United States reports that 80 percent of couples who marry before the age of eighteen end up divorced within five years.[1] It is important to let your teenager know that marriage requires a great deal of work to communicate effectively, to resolve arguments, to designate marital responsibilities, and to stay close under pressure. To help your teenager determine whether to get married, have him or her again answer the questions on page 147, this time evaluating the responsibilities of being a husband or wife rather than those of being a parent.

Adoption and Foster Care

The third alternative is for the baby to be given up to be raised by another couple. This can be done either through adoption or foster care. Adoption is permanent. The adoptive couple will legally become the child's parents, and your teenager will have to give up all parental rights. Foster care is a temporary situation, in which the child is raised by foster parents until one or both of the natural parents is ready to permanently care for him. Foster care should be considered by a teenager only if he or she expects to be able to assume the responsibility for child rearing within a short period of time.

Giving a child up for adoption can be an enormous sacrifice for a mother to make. The maternal feelings that a woman has after giving birth may be very strong. It is not unusual for a mother to go into a period of mourning after giving up her child to another set of parents, as if someone close to her had died. Like abortion, the alternatives of adoption and foster care tend to be much more painful decisions for women than they are for men.

Your teenager can obtain a list of local or private agencies dealing in adoption and foster care by contacting an agency such as the Florence Crittenton Association or Planned Parenthood (both listed in the appendix).

It's Not Over Yet

Baseball great Yogi Berra once said, "It's not over 'til it's over." That may apply to sporting events, but when dealing with teen pregnancies, it's not over even after it's over. Whether your teenager was actually involved in a pregnancy or whether it turned out to be a false alarm, this is not a time when you can simply take a deep sigh of relief and say "I'm glad that's over with." The only thing that is over is the immediate emergency. There is still another problem at hand. You now know with certainty that your teenager is engaging in intercourse, and that most likely he or she does not have all the facts straight about contraception. If you don't give your adolescent some very clear messages right now, your family may be in for further pregnancies down the line. Just because teenagers have endured the trauma of one pregnancy does not mean they will take the precautions necessary to avoid future pregnancies.

If you haven't already done so, read chapter 15 and take

the recommended steps for dealing with a sexually active teenager. Even if your son or daughter swears up and down that he or she has learned a painful lesson and will never have sex again until married, *don't back off.* Teenagers are victims of their hormones. Even with the best of intentions, they frequently get carried away in the heat of the moment. You will sleep better at night if you know that your teenager has both the knowledge and the preparedness to deal safely with future sexual encounters.

17

DEALING WITH SEXUAL TRAUMA

This chapter is for the parents of any teenager who has been forced to engage in any kind of sex. Whether the sex acts were a result of physical force, intimidation, or verbal coercion; whether they were committed by a date, a friend, a relative, or a complete stranger, your teenager is a victim of sexual assault.

Unfortunately, the number of sexual assaults in our society is staggering. In one survey of college women, it was found that more than one-half had experienced sexual aggression at some time.[1] In another survey of teenagers, 14 percent of the girls reported they had been raped.[2] If your teenager is unfortunate enough to endure any form of sexual assault, there are a number of things you can do that will help you and your teenager minimize the trauma.

Dealing with the Trauma

As with other very personal incidents, teens are often extremely reluctant to tell their parents if they have been sexually assaulted. You might find out about it from another source. But no matter how you come by this knowledge, it is crucial that you take immediate steps to deal with the situation. As a clinical psychologist, I deal with victims who have recently experienced a sexual assault and others who suffered their sexual traumas years or even decades ago. One fact that clearly emerges from every one of the victims is that *the psychological scars of sexual trauma have as much to do with the way the trauma is handled by the family, police, and counselors as they do with the trauma itself.*

The following are a number of recommendations for lessening the psychological and physical scars caused by sexual assault. Some are intended to be implemented immediately while others may be more appropriate over the course of time.

Immediate Steps

1. In cases of rape or other physical violence, immediately take your teenager for medical attention, preferably to a hospital emergency room. Do not clean her up; advise her not to change her clothes before going to the hospital, as uncomfortable as that may be. It will be important in collecting evidence for later prosecution of the perpetrator.

Medical treatment for your teenager is important not only to ensure that no serious physical injuries have occurred, but also to take the necessary steps to prevent a pregnancy and to minimize the possibility of getting sexually transmitted diseases. Offer to be present during physical examinations or during any investigatory questioning. But if your teenager expresses a need for confidentiality and privacy, respect those wishes.

2. Call your local rape crisis center (check under "Rape"

in both the yellow and white pages). Many centers will send a counselor to the emergency room to assist you.

3. If there is any thought of prosecuting, it is best to call the police immediately. Many of the details will be less clear after a while. The longer the delay in reporting a sexual assault, the less the chance of successfully prosecuting the crime.

4. Both parents must be openly and unconditionally supportive of the victim. If one parent is supportive, and the other is silent, teenagers will often interpret the silence as condemnation.

5. Let your teenager know that you are there for her. A hug, some physical comforting, and the knowledge that you love her can be very important tools of rehabilitation. Let her know that you will protect her to the best of your ability.

6. There must be no accusations, recriminations, or "I told you so"s. If your teenager was forced to engage in any sexual activity or was in any way traumatized in a sexual engagement, she is a victim. Sometimes teenagers are reluctant to be open with parents because the truth is they were at places they were not supposed to be or doing things they know their parents would not approve of. Let them know that you are on their side unconditionally.

7. Allow your teenager her feelings. Do not try to stop her from crying or being sad or angry. If she turns those feelings against herself (in guilt, self-hatred, etc.), just be supportive and assure her that no matter what her actions were, there are absolutely no circumstances when it is right or "understandable" for one person to abuse or traumatize another. Guilt is a very common emotion after a sexual assault. Reiterate to your teenager that no matter what she did, sexual assault is never a justifiable consequence.

8. Be a good listener. Do not try to impose your concerns or your feelings on your teenager. You can express your

concerns, but remember, you are there for her. Her concerns are an important priority.

9. Confirm the obvious. Let her know you understand that she is in a great deal of pain and how hurtful it is to be forced into anything. Many teens try to play down how the trauma has affected them or feel that they have overreacted to the situation. It is extremely important for them to understand that any sexual abuse is a major injustice. There is nothing trivial about being forced into a sexual encounter.

Later Steps

10. Do not force your child into revealing the details of the trauma until she is ready. However, it is extremely important that she speak to someone. If she is unwilling to talk to you about the trauma, make sure she has some other adult she can be open with (e.g., a rape crisis counselor, a psychologist, a pastor). Many victims of sexual assault find it especially helpful to talk with someone who has experienced something similar.

11. If the information about the assault came directly from your teenager, let her know you appreciate that she trusted you. If it did not, let her know that you would like her to trust you, but don't chastise her for not coming to you. Be supportive. Try to understand why she might have been reluctant to tell you.

12. It is extremely important to reiterate that sex is meant to be loving, not painful. Let your teenager know that sex can be tender and enjoyable and that what has occurred should not color her future sexual expectations. In addition, let her know that not all sexual partners will behave in such an abusive way, that loving partners are the norm, not the exception, and that she is deserving of a loving partner. If

the assault came from a friend or date, confirm that she has a right and an obligation to say "no" and to set her own limits in any sexual relationship.

13. Assist your teenager in finding a counselor who has dealt with this kind of trauma. Ask a physician or therapist you trust for recommendations, or call a rape crisis center. Contact the counselor yourself before your teenager's first appointment and ask about his or her credentials and experience in this area of counseling. Keep shopping until you find one that you believe has the proper credentials as well as the empathy and sensitivity required for this situation.

14. Help with some of the difficult decisions your child faces, such as reporting the incident to the police and possible legal proceedings. A rape crisis center can be very helpful in evaluating the alternatives. Staff members will be familiar with the training and reputation of your local police and law enforcement authorities in dealing with victims of sexual assault.

The final decision belongs to your teen. If, however, you think that your teenager, because of her emotional state, is not making effective decisions regarding her health and welfare, you may have to step in.

15. Assist in any crisis related to religious beliefs that may occur. Help her find a clergyman who can assist her through her religious crisis. Speak to the clergyman yourself before recommending that she go, just to get a feeling of how he may react. Some clergymen are overzealous or overcritical. Not all are equally competent at this type of counseling.

16. Do not treat the sexual assault as an unspeakable secret. That only conveys to your teenager the underlying message that there is something she should be ashamed of. There need be no shame or embarrassment. She has been

the victim of a crime, a physical assault. In addition, treating the assault as a shameful secret will make it difficult for either you or your teenager to get support from friends and family.

17. Don't neglect your own crisis. Many parents feel they have failed. Don't blame yourself any more than you would blame your child. If you can be less self-critical, you can be of more assistance to your teen. Do not hesitate to seek counseling for yourself.

Incest

As difficult as it is to deal with any sexual assault, even more difficult for most families is dealing with the trauma of incest. Incest is any overtly sexual contact between people who are closely related, either by blood or by family circumstance (including stepparents, stepsiblings, half-siblings, and even parents' lovers if they have assumed a family role).[3] This does *not* refer to minor sexual contacts between preteen brothers and sisters, which are initiated to satisfy a natural curiosity through mutual exploration. It has been estimated that this type of innocent sex play between siblings takes place in as many as nine out of ten families with more than one child. Such situations should certainly be discouraged, but handled tactfully and with understanding; situations that involve no coercion often require no counseling and certainly no legal intervention.

When an incestual relationship is uncovered, the trauma and disruption to the family are much more complicated than in a nonincestuous sexual assault. The family has not only the responsibility of supporting the victim but also the burden of having a family member who may face criminal charges. This becomes even more difficult if the perpetrator is also the breadwinner in the family. On top of everything, the family must face both the silent accusations and emotionally charged responses of friends and relatives. The following excerpt from an actual court case in California demonstrates clearly how emotionally loaded the topic of incest is in our society. Although the verbalizations of the judge are not typical courtroom behavior and the judge was duly censured, the attitudes that the judge displayed toward the boy at fault indicate the depth of emotion that is aroused *toward the whole family* when the taboo of incest is violated in our society:

The Court: I don't have much hope for you. You will probably end up in State's Prison before you are 25, and that's where you belong, anyhow. There is nothing much you can do.

I think you haven't got any moral principles. You won't acquire anything. Your parents won't teach you what is right or wrong and won't watch out.

Apparently, your sister is pregnant; is that right?
The Minor's Father, Mr. XXXXX: Yes.
The Court: It's a fine situation. How old is she?
The Minor's Mother, Mrs. XXXXX: Fifteen.
The Court: Well, probably she will have a half a dozen children and three or four marriages before she is 18.

The county will have to take care of you. You are no particular good to anybody. We ought to send you out of the country.[4]

Often, parents are unaware of incest going on in their home because they close their eyes to the possibility and refuse to acknowledge or give voice to their own fears and concerns. In many cases the abused child tells a parent only to be chastised for lying or making up stories.

If you even suspect that your child is being molested or has been molested by a member of your family, you must immediately talk with that child and seek professional counseling. If your child comes to you and tells you that he or she is being molested, *believe it*. Children *very rarely* make up such stories. The few children who do are still sending a message that they need help. Immediately call a rape crisis center and seek counseling. Do not hesitate.

If incest is occurring in your household, you have two choices: either you immediately go for professional and legal help to protect your child, or you become a silent partner in the molestation. There are no other options.

If you choose to maintain the secret rather than seek assistance, your whole family will gradually be destroyed. You will begin to suffer under the weight of your feelings of guilt and inadequacy.

If you choose to maintain the secret, your child will continue to endure all the pain of a rape plus the even greater pain of a betrayal in which trust has been totally shattered. She will know that her body and her well-being are being bartered for a sick peace within the family.

If you choose to maintain the secret, the abusing family member will be allowed to continue his sexual assaults, all the while feeling out of control, as if his whole world may crumble at any minute. He too will be deprived of the chance to get help.

If you choose to maintain the secret, any other children at home will be exposed to the risk of being molested.

Psychological treatment for an incest victim, and for the whole family, is a necessity. The psychological damage is often considerably greater and deeper than that suffered by victims of nonincestuous sexual assault. Unlike the victim of rape, the incest victim does not have the luxury of taking refuge with friends and family. "There is no stranger to run from, no home to run to. The child cannot feel safe in his or her own bed."[5] It is a terrible, terrifying feeling to be so alone.

18

IF YOU'RE A SINGLE PARENT

Life as a single parent is different than it is for a parent in a functioning marriage. Not necessarily better, not necessarily worse; just different. Likewise, for the children of divorced, separated, widowed, or never-married singles, the experiences of life are different than they might be if both parents were rearing them in the same household. Again, not necessarily better or worse, just different.

Even with regard to their sexuality and sex education, children of single parents are in a different situation from their friends who live with both parents. Not as far as the basic information these youths require but with regard to the influences that shape their sexuality and their sexual values. In a survey of American teenagers, Robert Coles and Geoffrey Stokes found that those "whose parents are divorced or separated are much more likely to have had intercourse than those whose parents are married or widowed."

	Married	Separated	Divorced	Widowed
Nonvirgins	26%	40%	49%	32%
Virgins	74	60	51	68

159

Further, they found that teenagers of divorced and separated parents more enthusiastically endorsed the idea of couples living together before marriage.[1]

	Married	Separated	Divorced	Widowed
OK to live together	50%	63%	69%	57%
Not OK to live together	50	37	31	43

If you are one of the more than twelve million singles in the United States who face the daily responsibilities of custodial parenthood, or if you are a noncustodial parent, this chapter can help you understand how to deal with your teenager's sexuality.

Differences Are Not Necessarily Disadvantages

It is difficult to predict what differences you as a single parent may experience in raising your teenagers or, for that matter, the differences your teen may experience in being raised. Every single-parent family is unique. However, there are some issues that occur frequently enough in single-parent households to deserve specific mention. For some families these issues may eventually create problems, whereas for others they may simply lead to learning opportunities not experienced by two-parent families.

What follows are some glances at these issues and some suggested ways you can minimize any negative influences. Be realistic in assessing what changes you might make. Recognize that you are only human and that your time, your emotional resources, and your finances are limited. Just do the best you can.

Your Time as a Parent Is Scarce

In addition to parenting, you need to ration your time for work, coordinating the household, organizing your finances, handling emergencies, seeing family and friends, and dating, and still find enough private time to maintain your sanity. Whereas a couple can share all the household responsibilities along with the responsibilities of parenting, in a single household they all fall on the shoulders of the custodial parent. This means that your teenager may not get as much of your time as you would like to give.

Set aside some time every day or a few times each week just for the two of you. If you have more than one child, set separate time aside for each one. Do not expect to find time spontaneously to be with each child. Your crowded schedule and theirs will usually not accommodate that. Plan with your teenager how to use your time together effectively. The message you will be communicating is a very important one: that your teenager is a priority.

This can also help reduce problems that may come up when you date. One of the most frequent reasons a child feels threatened by a parent's dating is that it lessens the time the parent has available to nurture him. The child then feels in competition with the date for the parent's time. If you let your teenager know by your actions that time with him is a priority, his feelings of jealousy are likely to be reduced.

Making Decisions Is Difficult

As a parent, I know that making decisions about my teenager's welfare is difficult. No matter what I decide, one or the other of my teenagers doesn't seem to like it. It is really comforting to have the feedback and/or support of another adult when making an important decision (especially regarding teenagers, who seem to think that their life hangs on every decision). As a single parent, you do not have that luxury. You must make all, or at least a great many, parental decisions without having a spouse to talk the issues through with.

You can find that helpful support in other adults, particularly parents who have children about the age of yours or slightly older. Sometimes a support group of other single parents can be a big help (although it may be hard to find one). Check with groups such as Parents Without Partners or your local family service agency. At the very least, seek out friends who have teenagers so that you can get their feedback about your decision making.

Since many parental decisions are spur-of-the-moment ones, you may not have the leisure to fully evaluate all the issues before you blurt out your answer. Recognize that your decision making will not be perfect. Just do the best you can, and learn from those decisions that do not work out the way you want them to. If you are divorced, do not make decisions simply because you know they will upset your former spouse. Make decisions because you are comfortable with them.

Grieving the Loss of One Parent, Fearing the Loss of the Other

All children are affected by the loss of a parent, some more deeply than others. Whether that loss occurs through separation, divorce, or death, the process is very much the same. Grieving is a natural part of adjusting to a lost parent, and it can continue for months or even years.

Allow your child to grieve. Even if you are angry or at war with your former spouse, allow your child to feel the loss. If it is difficult for you to listen to your child express feelings of sadness or loss for his absent parent, don't be afraid to say so. You are also going through a tough time, and it's OK for your children to know that. If it is hard for you to be supportive, you can suggest another person he can talk with or arrange for counseling.

Having felt the loss of one parent, your teenager may have conscious or unconscious fears of losing you as well. This is often exacerbated when you begin to date or become more serious about a new relationship. Ask your teenager directly if he has any such fears and encourage him to talk openly about them. Reassure him that you have no intention of leaving the family and demonstrate that by your actions as well as your words.

What They See Is What You Get

Like most of us, teenagers learn more from the examples you set than from the words you say. Any gap between what you say and what you do will immediately undermine your credibility. With single parents, nowhere is this more true than in the category of dating and sexuality.

Whereas married parents can simply verbalize what their standards are and hope that their teenager adheres to them, a single parent is likely to become a model of those very standards. As a single parent, you have a unique opportunity to actually set an example for your teenager in the areas of dating and sexuality. When your teenager sees you dating, he has a living demonstration of what dating and sexuality are all about. Be certain that the values you want to impart to your child can be honestly reconciled with the values you demonstrate. Your words, your actions, even the tone of your voice will set an example for your teenager. Everything about your dating habits—including how you treat your partners, how you talk about them, and such decisions as who spends the night and how open you are about your sexuality—are all subject to scrutiny.

Likewise, your dating, or even your lack of dating, gives you a unique appreciation of your teen's social life. Your own experiences will give you the opportunity to openly discuss dating, sex, and sexual feelings. Use it to your advantage. In this respect, at least, you have it easier than parents who live together.

That is not to say that your own feelings will be completely straightforward. Many singles find themselves grappling with their own sexuality at the same time that their teenager is dealing with his. As a single parent who is either dating already or facing the challenge of dating, you will be confronted by your own sexual values, as well as those of potential partners. Make sure your behaviors are consistent with your belief system. If you are confused about your own sexuality, seek counseling. It will be difficult for you to affirm a positive attitude about sex if you are unclear about your own sexual values or actions. Develop a moral standard that is comfortable for you and, at the same time, is consistent with what you wish to communicate to your teen. Be particularly clear on one point: Would you be comfortable if your children, when they become adults, exhibit the same sexual behavior as you do now? If not, why?

That brings us to an important point. Your life-style includes a lot of behavior that is appropriate for you as an adult but which would not be appropriate for your teen. If you believe that adults have the right to live by different sexual standards than do teens, bring this up for discussion. Teenagers will note all discrepancies whether you verbalize them or not. Your teenager may disagree with what is in effect a double standard, but at least you will have given him the opportunity for open discussion. Realize, however, that your teenager may follow your role model rather than your words. Consequently your discussion may not have the impact you wish it could.

The Missing Role Model

Many single parents, particularly those with a child of the opposite gender, worry about the void their teenager faces in the absence of an adequate role model. Frequently, the parent fears that lacking a role model of the same gender, their teenager will become homosexual, feel sexually inadequate, or in some other way manifest a lack of conviction of their masculinity or femininity. The reality is that the absence of a parent as a role model *is* a significant loss. Ordinarily, both parents provide important models of maleness and femaleness. However, even in the absence of one parent, you can provide much of what your teen requires. You can provide a positive model of what it means to be a healthy, sexual adult. And, by discussing the positive and negative aspects of models provided by adult friends, family members, TV or movie personalities, and even the missing parent, your teenager can begin to evolve his or her own sense of gender identity.

Some teens handle the issues involved in being raised by a single parent without difficulty and, in fact, may utilize them as a springboard to independence. Others are adversely affected. Just remember that your teenager is not automatically at a disadvantage simply because you are a single parent. Whether you are male or female, and whether your teenager is of the same or the opposite gender, you are capable of raising him or her to become a confident and responsible sexual being.

19

THE HOMOSEXUAL
TEENAGER

This chapter is meant to help the parent whose teenager is convinced he is homosexual or is seriously confused about his sexual preference. Understand, however, that it can provide merely a beginning point to assist you in recognizing some of the critical issues involved and in coping with them in a constructive manner. Dealing with this situation will raise very complex and painful issues, well beyond the scope of this book. Parents should supplement this chapter with further reading and very possibly with psychological counseling.

Your teenager's thoughts and feelings about his homosexual orientation are not concepts that just recently popped into his mind. More than likely, his pronouncement occurred only after years of soul searching and agony. For some youngsters, the initial feelings of homosexuality first surface in early childhood, whereas for others, recognition begins in their teens. Some know before their first sexual encounter; others find out only after years of trying desperately to fit into a heterosexual role. For almost all, however, their struggle has involved years of feeling different from other kids, and years of suppressing emotions and thoughts. During that time they have heard their friends talking about fantasies and attraction toward the opposite sex, knowing they do not share these feelings and thoughts. They have been exposed to the same jokes and negative stereotypes about homosexuals as their friends but have absorbed them with a gnawing pain, knowing that these prejudices referred to them. In the world of adolescents, where so much depends on feeling approval and acceptance as one of the group, your adolescent has felt neither. He has felt different. He has felt alone. He has felt abnormal. He has felt diseased.

Fearing ridicule and rejection, your teenager has no doubt learned to conceal and censor. Almost certainly, he has hidden his feelings for years out of fear that no one would understand. Wayne V. Pawlowski, a clinical social worker who counsels gay youths, notes that "homosexual adolescents learn two crucial lessons early on. *Invisibility has its rewards.* If you do not inform anyone about what you feel, you will stay out of trouble. *Dishonesty is the key to close relationships.* The way to keep friends and family close and to avoid their rejection is to be dishonest about your feelings, thoughts, and needs."[1]

Dealing with the News

The initial reaction of many parents to finding out about their teenager's homosexual feelings is absolute shock, followed by self-concern. If your teenager has shared with you realizations or concerns about homosexual feelings, chances are that you are experiencing grief, shame, and guilt, along with thoughts of "Where have I gone wrong?" and "What will my friends think?" It is natural and normal to feel the pain and concern for yourself, but in doing so, don't forget your child's pain. Make sure that you do not become a part of his problem. In fact, if you take only one thought from this chapter, let it be this: *Become part of the solution to your teenager's dilemma, not part of the problem.*

After your initial reaction, try to realize that your child has probably spent many excruciating years wrestling with an incredible dilemma, and will probably face many more years of prejudice and discrimination. Recognize, also, that along with the pain that you and your adolescent are feeling, there is some good news: your teenager has an incredible amount of trust in you. Many gays acknowledge that having to face their parents and admit their sexual preference is considerably more difficult than the task of coming to terms with it themselves. If your teenager has shared his sexual preference with you, he is demonstrating tremendous trust. This can provide an excellent foundation for establishing a new feeling of closeness and solidarity within your family.

Understanding What Homosexuality Is, and What It Is Not

A homosexual is a person whose primary means of receiving sexual pleasure is with members of his own sex. Homosexuality is not a disease; it is not even a life-style. Homosexuals have one thing in common: a preference for a sexual partner of the same gender. Some gays maintain a life-style that involves close alignment and identification with the homosexual community, whereas others forego the community affiliation or gay identification and keep their sexual orientation private. If your teenager believes he is or may

169

be homosexual, it is essential that you get as much information as possible to understand what homosexuality is, and what it is not. Chapter 13 reviews some of the common myths and stereotypes about homosexuality, but again, further reading is recommended (see the bibliography).

At one time it was believed that homosexuality was caused by a combination of a strong, dominating mother and a weak or nonexistent father. Studies have demonstrated that families with this combination of parents are no more likely to have a homosexual child than any other parental combination. At the present time the causes of homosexuality remain unknown.

Coming Out

The process of publicly acknowledging one's homosexuality is commonly called "coming out." If your youth wants to "come out," discourage him from doing so prematurely, but don't try to talk him out of his homosexuality. It may, in fact, be right for him. If you can, acknowledge this possibility. Even joining gay organizations may be the right decision, but at the appropriate time. It is important that he keep his options open. You will not be able to prevent your teenager's "coming out" if this is what he is determined to do. But he should be urged not to make a hasty decision to go public with his homosexuality until he has thoroughly explored the consequences. (In addition, he should be encouraged to follow the three steps mentioned in the next section.)

Although acknowledging a homosexual orientation may be a necessary stage of growth for the teenager, to make this public knowledge is asking for discrimination. Your child may mean it as an act of self-identity, but the results may include discrimination at school, in getting a job, in being accepted into certain schools, or being taken into the military. There is also the risk of being isolated by friends or other family members. At the extreme, homosexuals are sometimes treated as lepers by prejudiced or misinformed youths, particularly in the present confused atmosphere surrounding AIDS. Even friends and acquaintances who are accepting of homosexuality will probably demonstrate some discomfort and awkwardness toward your adolescent.

Resolving Feelings and Making Decisions

Any teenager who suspects that he may be gay has gone through, and will continue to go through, a great deal of fear and confusion. *A Way of Love, a Way of Life,* an excellent book for young people trying to understand what it means to be gay, suggests three main steps in trying to reach a feeling of resolution.

1. The teenager should take time to understand what he is feeling. It is not necessary for him to act impulsively or make immediate decisions.
2. The teenager should get as much information as possible from reliable sources. There are many excellent books about homosexuality. He should not rely on any single book or resource for his information, since this may present him with a very one-sided view.
3. The teenager should seek out an adult to talk with. It is up to him who that person will be, but whoever he chooses should be capable of listening and responding without attempting to bias the teenager toward one sexual orientation or another.[2]

The same three steps are equally applicable to parents who are trying to understand their own confusion about their teenager's sexual orientation. You, too, should not act hastily, should take time to understand your feelings, and should seek unbiased information and counseling.

Going for Counseling

If you seek counseling, recognize that therapists are human also. Although they are trained to counsel in a nonjudgmental way, they too have biases and prejudices. Whether you are seeking a therapist for the family or one for your adolescent, make sure he or she does not try to impose any biases about homosexuality. Choose a therapist who has considerable training and/or experience in dealing with individuals or families who are trying to sort out their feelings about homosexuality.

In your first visit with the therapist, state what your objectives are and listen to how he responds to them. If you are uncomfortable with something he says, confront him. If at the end of the session you feel that the therapist is too biased in one direction or the other, or if you find that he avoids dealing with the topic of homosexuality, change therapists. Likewise, if you or your teenager do not have trust in the therapist, shop around until you find someone who fits your needs.

It is essential that you and your teenager understand that the role of the therapist is not to make decisions or to push in any single direction. His job is to help each member of the family understand his own feelings and to make his own decisions. There is no guarantee that at the end of therapy, everyone will live happily ever after.

Dos and Don'ts

The following is a summary of the major "dos and don'ts" in dealing with your teenager's homosexuality or sexual confusion. The first ones to remember are these: As with any suggestions in this book, don't expect perfection in implementing them; however, do try to follow these guidelines as closely as possible.

Dos

- Become part of the solution, not part of the problem.
- Try to be nonjudgmental and accepting, but on the other hand, don't expect miracles from yourself. You too were raised with many myths and prejudices. It will take a while to get over them.
- Allow yourself to feel disappointed. We all have dreams for our children, and it is difficult when our dreams are shattered.
- Give yourself permission to feel whatever emotions you are feeling. It isn't your emotions that need to be curbed. It is the behavior that could follow the emotions. Allow yourself to feel angry, sad, hurt, and so on. Even allow yourself to express these emotions in a constructive manner.
- Understand that your teenager has had a very difficult adolescence and may be very lonely.
- Be loving. Seeing you as a loving parent will help your teenager to love himself.
- Understand that your teenager has a very difficult time ahead of him. Not only will he face the specters of prejudice, discrimination, and AIDS, but he must live in a society that to a large extent still views homosexuality as a disease.

173

- Appreciate that your teenager is exhibiting great courage and trust in sharing this with you.
- Be ready to listen. It is more important that you listen than speak.
- Encourage him to express his feelings. Recognize that some of these feelings may be directed at you and may be difficult to listen to. Do not get defensive, just listen and accept that right now this is the way he perceives things.
- Educate yourself and encourage your teenager to educate himself about homosexuality. Check the bibliography for references.
- Follow the rules of communication listed in chapter 6.
- Read Chapter 15, "The Sexually Active Teenager," very carefully.
- Recognize that homosexuals are capable of having a quality relationship with a same-sex partner.
- Encourage counseling to help your teenager make decisions and/or to adjust to his life-style.
- Know that you can love and accept your teenager even if you don't approve of his life-style.
- Discourage your teenager from "coming out" prematurely.

Don'ts

- Don't tell him not to worry. He most likely has had a great deal to worry about and will continue to face many obstacles.
- Don't treat him as though this is a phase he will grow out of. This is a major struggle for your teenager. He is in great pain.
- Don't say anything that can't be taken back. If you shoot off your mouth and regret it, apologize.
- Don't judge, condemn, or put your adolescent down. He

is searching for an identity. If you communicate that he is a bad or inadequate person, he will absorb this as part of his identity. You will not accomplish what you want.

- Don't indicate that your teenager has an emotional problem. If there is a problem, it may very well be yours (an inability to accept homosexuality as a sexual preference).
- Don't try to talk your teenager out of his homosexuality.
- Don't act as if this is a crime against you.
- Don't jump in and try to run his life. He must make the decisions for himself.
- Don't bother trying to figure out what you did wrong. This is an exercise in futility. You didn't make your child homosexual. You made some mistakes, just as *all* parents have. Basically, you did the best that you could.
- Don't suggest counseling in order to change your teenager's mind about being a homosexual. Counseling is recommended to clarify your adolescent's sexual preference, not to change it.

20

THE HANDICAPPED
TEENAGER

The objective of this chapter is to help parents of handicapped teenagers become aware of the sexual feelings and needs of their children and the alternatives available to them. Although some specific handicaps are mentioned, most of the content applies to teens and young adults with virtually any handicap: physical or mental. This chapter provides only a fraction of the information you will need in order to give your teen an adequate sex education. Remember that your child is first and foremost a teenager, with teenage needs and teenage feelings. Secondarily, he is handicapped. So before reading this chapter, thoroughly familiarize yourself with the information contained throughout this book. It is as relevant to your teenager as it is to the able-bodied teen.

Your Child Is Sexual

All of us are inherently sexual. Your teen is no exception. He has sexual needs, desires, and feelings. In addition, he has or will soon have a desire to love and be loved; not only by you, in a parental way, but also by a mate, a lover, a friend. He has sexual thoughts and sexual fantasies. He is a sexual being. Sexuality is a natural and wonderful part of being human, and it is important that he learn to appreciate this part of himself.

Because of certain limitations that your child has, you may need to serve as a bridge between him and sexual fulfillment. Consequently the way you perceive your teenager and his sexuality is crucial. Many parents of handicapped adolescents try to screen their children from information about sexuality under the mistaken notion that they are protecting them from hurt. This lack of information serves only to magnify the problem. If you define your child as asexual, it makes him feel that somehow the urges he experiences are aberrant, and confirms even more solidly in his mind that he is incapable of a loving, sexual relationship. Rehabilitation must include all aspects of a handicapped person's life, and this includes sexuality. Certainly the process for being sexual may be somewhat different for a handicapped person than it is for an able-bodied one. Thus your teenager needs encouragement to explore and to be inventive so that he can express the full range of his sexuality.

Assessing the Situation

When preparing your adolescent to be a sexual person, the first thing you have to do is assess his situation to determine which physical or mental obstacles are likely to impede his progress, and then to think through a game plan to help him deal with them. Begin by folding a piece of paper in half. Place the heading "potential problems" on the left side of the page and the heading "possible solutions" on the right side. As you read this chapter, list any of the impediments you think might restrict your adolescent's sexuality. If you think of any others that have not been included, put them on your list as well. You don't have to be certain about an item to include it on your list; you can always delete it later. Simply list everything you think might create even a slight problem for your child. Finally, consider some of the possible solutions and list any that seem appropriate for your teenager on the right side of your page.

The Secondary Handicap

Ironically, relatively few handicapped people are prevented from being sexual by their primary physical disability. Often, their sexuality is more severely restricted by a number of secondary problems that are only indirectly a result of their impairment. The following is a list of some of these problems:

Psychological Barriers

Assuming a handicapped mentality—Some of the handicapped give up on their abilities and focus primarily on their limitations. There is a significant difference between being physically handicapped and assuming a handicapped mentality.

Boredom—Because of their physical restrictions and/or social isolation, many handicapped kids become bored. This can be a significant problem, since bored people can be very boring and are often viewed as unattractive partners.

Depression—Because of any or all of these barriers, youths may enter a state of psychological depression. Although many parents associate depression with sadness or despondency, often this is not the case. Probably the greatest single sign of psychological depression is a feeling of apathy and detachment, an absence of feeling.

Embarrassment—Handicapped youths often feel a sense of embarrassment or shame about their handicap.

Feelings of unattractiveness—Many of the handicapped, particularly the physically handicapped, tend to view themselves as physically unattractive. In one study of 111 physically handicapped respondents, 41 percent felt that their handicap made them sexually unattractive.[1]

Physical Barriers

Catheters, braces, et cetera—These may either physically limit the handicapped person or create psychological barriers.

Lack of verbal ability—Because communication is an essential part of sex, lack of verbal ability can create some very real roadblocks.

Medications, drugs, and alcohol—Any chemical placed inside the body will have both main effects and side effects. Many medications, as well as the use of drugs or alcohol, can significantly alter the physical and/or the psychological aspects of sexual experiences.

Personal hygiene—This can be significant, both because personal hygiene may be harder for the handicapped person to maintain, and because of the fear many physically disabled youths have that they will suffer an intestinal or bladder accident.

Social Barriers

Isolation—Although few handicapped youth are absolutely isolated from society, lack of mobility or lack of ready access to transportation makes isolation more of a significant factor than it might be for the able-bodied.

Lack of friends—Even with social opportunities, some handicapped teens lack the skills or the confidence to make friends. This deprives the teenager of both the opportunity to discuss his feelings with others and the opportunity to eventually find a sexual partner.

Societal prejudices—This is an unfortunate reality that most handicapped people experience.

Understanding the Primary Handicap

The following pages discuss some of the common sexual limitations experienced by teens who are motor handicapped, mentally retarded, deaf, or blind. Not all of the limitations discussed nor all of the suggested solutions will apply to your teenager. Since every handicapped person experiences his limitations differently, the best way to get a clear impression of your adolescent's sexual handicap is to ask questions and discuss the problem. Discuss it with him, his physician, his counselors, and anyone else who can shed some light on his restrictions. With each discussion, use your list as a starting point, adding additional "potential problems" and "possible solutions" as you proceed.

The Motor Handicapped Teenager

In D. H. Lawrence's classic novel *Lady Chatterley's Lover*, Lord Chatterley, a paraplegic invalid, is described as being impotent (unable to get an erection), with the implication that his wife's love affairs are a natural consequence of his sexual inability. It is this unfortunate image of sexual impotency and asexuality that has become a stereotype for the motor handicapped, not only for men, but for women as well.

> Most able bodied women experience problems in being treated as a *sexual object* whereas many disabled women experience being treated as an *asexual object*. The experience of the able bodied woman can be devastating in feelings or social status, but being treated as asexual can be even more so.[2]

In reality, there is no reason to believe that the sex drive of motor disabled people is any lower than that of comparably aged, able-bodied people. Many male paraplegics and quadriplegics do face problems of impotency caused by their physical disability, by some of the secondary factors listed above, or by other difficulties unrelated to their handicap. However, because of advances in both the psychological and the medical treatment of impotency, there is absolutely no reason that inability to attain or sustain an erection should be a major factor in preventing any couple from enjoying a sexual relationship. In situations where the problem is psychological, therapy by a certified sex therapist has been found to be extremely effective. In situations where sex therapy fails, or in physiologically based sexual dysfunctions, various medical interventions, including surgical implantation of an inflatable or semi-rigid prosthesis, can virtually ensure a male that he will be able to attain an erection.

Sexual intimacy and petting for the motor handicapped person require considerably more experimentation and planning, including the possible use of vibrators or other sexual aids. Your child needs the encouragement to be creative and imaginative. In addition, he needs specific instruction about possible sexual positions. A wonderful book for teenagers who are ready for the material is *Sexual Options for Paraplegics and Quadriplegics*, by Mooney, Cole, and Chilgren.[3] This book provides practical information about sexual positions and techniques that can be used during sex play and intercourse, including information on handling catheters, stomas, and so on. Most important, this book tells the handicapped person that sex is a possibility, despite his physical disadvantages.

Another important resource is the wide variety of films concerning sexuality and the physically handicapped. They can provide the handicapped youth with both the education he needs and the encouragement that sexuality can be a fulfilling part of his life.

The Mentally Retarded Teenager

Probably the greatest drawback to the sexual education of the mentally retarded is that they are often regarded as children throughout their lives. Although the mental capacity of a retarded teenager is limited, and he is slow to learn, his body and his sexual urges continue to mature as they would in most teenagers.

Interestingly, one of the reasons retarded teenagers are often shielded from information about sex is that their parents or caretakers believe not providing information will avoid arousing sexual curiosity or interest. Nothing could be farther from the truth! Retarded teenagers need more information about sex, not less. They possess the same sexual feelings and impulses as anyone else but are not exposed to the network of information and resources that fully functioning teens enjoy. In addition, they are much more at risk to be sexually abused than are their mentally able counterparts.

That is why contraception should be an extremely high priority with mentally retarded youth. Methods of birth control that need minimum supervision, such as birth control pills, should be given greatest consideration.

Many people think that sterilization of the mentally retarded is the way to stop sexual problems from arising. The only thing that sterilization prevents is pregnancy. It does not thwart the abuse of mentally retarded youths. It does not give them information that will allow them to differentiate public behavior from private behavior. And, most important, it does not grant them their birthright: to enjoy a loving sexual relationship with another person. Certainly sterilization may be appropriate for some mentally retarded youths, but this decision should be made on a case-by-case basis and only after carefully weighing all the medical, emotional, and practical considerations.

It is important to realize that the term "mental retardation" has very broad meaning and encompasses many different levels of functioning. At the top of the range are the mildly mentally retarded who are very able to control sexual impulses and deal with them as effectively as most teenagers. They tend to respond well to verbal modes of sex education and counseling. Many, if not most, of the mildly retarded are capable of having fulfilling and meaningful sexual relationships.

At the other end of the spectrum are those teenagers who are profoundly retarded. They function at a very basic level, having their immediate needs met. They are extremely impulsive, sexually and otherwise, and will often masturbate in ways that are harmful to themselves. At this level, there is really no effective form of verbal education. But the profoundly mentally retarded can at the very least be taught, through primary forms of reward and punishment, not to hurt themselves and what behaviors are appropriately private.

Obviously, many mentally retarded teenagers fall between these two extremes. For each of them, a special look at his abilities and disabilities is necessary. Some learn well through verbal instruction, others through different levels of reward and punishment. Some understand the social consequences of various actions, others do not.

In teaching the mentally retarded teenager about sex, it is important to keep communication and learning materials to a level he can understand. Stimulate as many different senses as possible during the education process, especially the auditory, visual, and tactile. Use films, books, anatomically correct dolls (dolls with genitals), and verbal discussion. And, most important, be repetitive.

The Visually Impaired Teenager

Obviously, the visually impaired teenager's problem is not the direct effects of his handicap upon sexual performance. The singular disadvantage a visually impaired person does have during a sexual encounter is the absence of the added arousal that visual stimulation provides. This, however, can be easily compensated for by an emphasis on tactility and verbal feedback during sexual encounters.

Rather, the most severe limitation for visually impaired teens is their restricted access to sex education materials (most of which are visual). To compensate, you can encourage open discussions, read books aloud, or record books into a tape recorder. Illustrations can be replaced by dolls with genitals or by anatomical models like the ones physicians keep in their offices. Don't hesitate to ask your doctor if he or she has such a model you could borrow or where you might find one.

The Hearing-Impaired Teenager

Although the deaf do not suffer a great disadvantage in learning about sexuality, they do endure the same secondary impediments as other handicapped teens. Such issues as social isolation and setting limits with their partners may be particularly relevant. In addition, since the verbal feedback during sex can be an important part of the trial-and-error learning process, it is important that once a deaf youth becomes sexually active, he be encouraged to communicate with his partner immediately after sexual encounters. In this way he can learn to assess his partner's likes and dislikes and to promote a process of feedback between partners.

Opening a Discussion

Before evaluating the list you have prepared and implementing a plan of action, it is important to discuss frankly with your teenager your concerns, your feelings, and your thoughts. If you feel incapable of directing such an open discussion, have a counselor present as a facilitator. Try not to dump this responsibility onto the counselor, however. Your input as a parent is important. The list you have prepared is a perfect starting point with which to open a discussion about sexuality. Use it to begin talking about what you believe to be your child's sexual limitations as well as what you view to be the sexual possibilities available to him. Be realistic. Don't overprotect and don't encourage situations that are certain to end for him in a feeling of defeat.

It would be worthwhile to share with him the following excerpt from *Raising a Child Conservatively in a Sexually Permissive World*, by Sol Gordon, Ph.D., and Judith Gordon, M.S.W. Use this, too, to stimulate further discussion about his sexuality. Since understanding and acting upon some of these points require considerable insight and the ability to envision alternatives, parents of mentally retarded youths may need to reword or entirely omit some things.

Here are a few messages for people who have handicaps, especially those who are feeling sorry for themselves.

In our society you score no points for being disabled. Every person who has a disability has to struggle to make it.

1. Nobody can make you feel inferior without your consent.
2. If you have an interest (hobbies, work, talents, passions) someone will be interested in you.
3. If you are bored, you are boring to be with.
4. If you do not have a sense of humor, cultivate one.
5. Join an advocacy group for the handicapped.
6. Do not dwell on the meaning of life. Life is not a meaning. Life is an opportunity for any number of meaningful experiences.
7. Read. Discover as much as you can about yourself and the world. For heaven's sake, do not watch more than a couple of hours of television each day. Haven't you noticed that the more television you watch, the more exhausted you are?
8. Operate on the assumption that the so-called general public is uncomfortable with you. Most people are uncomfortable in the presence of people who have handicaps. Usually, if you tell them they do not have to feel guilty about feeling uncomfortable, they will respond.

We feel that these "rules" are the basic steps toward realizing your own goals. Nothing we have suggested is easy. In fact, all really meaningful experiences in life involve risk, hard work and the ability to postpone momentary gratification for long-range satisfaction. If you are able to feel good about yourself, someone will feel good about you. If you feel friendly, someone will be friendly to you. If you are open to sexual expression, someone will want to be sexual with you.[4]

If you believe that your teenager is not emotionally or intellectually capable of handling such a discussion, speak to a counselor or therapist. The list you have written can provide a good groundwork for a discussion with the counselor about your adolescent's sexuality.

Learning About Conception, Contraception, and Sterilization

Having information about conception, contraception, and sterilization can be even more important for handicapped teenagers than for able-bodied teens. Not only do handicapped youths face the same concerns and risks about pregnancy and sexually transmitted diseases that others do, but they have some additional concerns:

1. Because of their physical or mental limitations, many handicapped couples find it difficult to care for an infant or child and may find the responsibility overwhelming.
2. For some handicapped women, the process of labor and delivery can be life threatening. (Whether this danger exists for your child can easily be ascertained by consulting a physician.)
3. Some handicapped women need to be especially con-

cerned about the type of contraception they use, either because their periods are irregular or because their handicap makes certain types of contraception difficult to use or unreliable.

4. Some handicaps are genetically determined and can be passed from one generation to the next. For a handicapped parent, the responsibility for caring for a handicapped child can be overwhelming. If pregnancy is a consideration and there is some doubt about the handicap being genetic, a geneticist should be consulted.

On the other hand, many handicapped youngsters are interested in eventually becoming parents and will be very capable of fulfilling that role when the time comes. If you believe that your adolescent may fall into this category, openly discuss any risks you are aware of or concerns that you have. If you anticipate that conception will be a problem or an impossibility, discuss other alternatives such as adoption and artificial insemination.

Opening Up to New Relationships

Being the parent of a handicapped teenager is an awesome responsibility. There are days you feel overwhelmed by how much there is to do and days when you feel guilty that you are not doing enough. Many parents of severely handicapped youths fear that opening the doors to sexuality will double the already enormous emotional, financial, and physical responsibilities by encouraging their teenager to enter a relationship with another handicapped youth.

The other side of the coin, however, is that opening his eyes to other relationships gives your teenager a chance to grow and can reduce much of your emotional burden. If he does eventually get married, you will get satisfaction from seeing your child enjoying a loving relationship, and any resources that his spouse or his spouse's caretaker bring to the relationship may also lighten your physical and financial responsibilities.

Going for Counseling

Many kinds of psychological counseling are available. Ideally, try to find a counselor who is a psychologist, who has training in the area of sexuality, and who has specialized training and experience with the handicapped. Recognize, however, that this is a tall order. Not all psychologists have experience with the handicapped, and of those who do, many are untrained or uncomfortable in dealing with sexuality. More than likely, you will have to settle for someone who fits two of these three criteria. Group counseling with other handicapped teenagers is often best, because it exposes them to the fears and feelings of others and gives them the opportunity to learn and to practice new social skills.

If medication is involved, a psychiatrist or other physician trained in the psychological and sexual effects of various medications should be consulted. If drugs or alcohol are suspected, consult a counselor trained in the area of chemical dependency.

Finally, do not overlook the fact that you yourself may benefit from counseling. Many parents are so focused on their children, or so intent on committing their financial and emotional resources for that purpose, that they ignore their own needs. As a parent, you too need to be nourished. Give yourself permission to seek counseling or support when you need it.

AFTERWORD

There is no choice about whether you will teach your teenager about sex. You do it, by the very nature of being a parent. You teach by example. Everything your child sees you do and hears you say, prepares him for his adulthood. *You are a role model*, and therefore *you are a teacher*.

The only question is, are you willing to provide your teenager with the sex education that he needs to protect himself in this very dangerous world; to furnish him with a library of facts and a foundation of values that can neutralize the destructive myths and lessen his anxieties and ambivalent feelings?

Equipping your teenager with the tools to become a sexually adjusted adult will take a substantial effort. There will be no shortcuts or ways to make the process easy. It will sometimes be uncomfortable for you and will often challenge your values and make you assess your own upbringing. However, no matter how uncomfortable your own sexuality has been or how little information about sex you received as a teenager, there is no excuse for letting your teenager rattle around, absorbing the inaccurate and inadequate sex education that he will receive from friends and the media.

As Masters & Johnson, the well-known pioneers in human sexuality, said in an article about sex education: "How sad . . . when parents refuse needed sex information on the grounds that their children must never know any more about sex than they, the parents, do, especially when what they know—or don't know—has led to discomfort, disillusionment or even dysfunction in their own lives."[1]

You cannot be there to protect your child from each and every danger that he will encounter. However, you can provide him with the one tool that will help him to protect himself: *knowledge.*

APPENDIX
FINDING HELP

We all need help now and then. None of us is completely self-sufficient. Yet asking for help can sometimes be very difficult. Even admitting that problems are serious enough to require help may be hard to do.

If you find yourself in a situation that requires professional advice or assistance, competent help is usually available if you know how to find it. This appendix is designed to ease the difficulties often connected with finding proper professional help. It is divided into three parts.

1. Getting a referral from friends or professionals
2. Using the phone book to find help
3. Organizations

Getting a Referral from Friends or Professionals

Not all professionals are equally competent. Not all professionals have an equal amount of training in the specialty area that you need. And not all professionals are equally easy to relate to. Clearly there will be some professionals who will fit your needs better than others.

The first step in finding a good professional to suit your purposes is to assess exactly what your needs are. What is the problem that needs fixing? Once you have clarified that in your own mind, think of a professional you respect and trust who might know someone to refer you to. It might be your family doctor, a teacher, a clergyman, or someone else. If you can't think of a professional, think of a friend or anyone you know who may have faced the same or a similar problem and seems to have successfully resolved it. Consider whether you feel comfortable in sharing your basic problem with that person. If so, speak to him or her and ask for recommendations or advice.

Ask as many questions as possible and take down the names and numbers of any recommended resources. Even if he or she recommends a resource that is not exactly what you had in mind, copy the name and phone number. A competent professional or agency can refer you to other competent resources. For instance, if your friend highly recommends a specific psychologist, but you think that you and your teenager need pregnancy counseling, it might be worthwhile to call the psychologist and ask if he knows of any agencies or professionals who have expertise in the area of counseling pregnant teens.

Get as many recommendations as you can. If the names of certain professionals keep popping up, it is worth giving them a call. Just because you call does not obligate you to make an appointment. Ask about their expertise in the area you need, and do not hesitate to ask about their training and years of experience. A competent professional does not need to be defensive about his training or experience. If you feel good about your discussion, make an appointment. If not, keep searching or tell the professional about some of your misgivings. He may be able to respond to your apprehensions or refer you to someone else you might be more comfortable with.

Using the Phone Book to Find Help

Probably the easiest way to find help is to look in the front (or back) of your local phone directory for the listings of community services numbers or the city, county, state, and federal government offices. Look under the word that best describes the service you require. For example, if you are looking for information about pregnancy, look in the white pages under the word "pregnancy." If you are looking for birth control information, look under "birth control" or even under "sex." If you don't find the referral source that you need, look up Planned Parenthood or Family Service. Both of these are large national organizations with chapters in many towns and cities. Even if these organizations do not offer the type of service you need, it is likely that they can refer you to a place where you can get appropriate help.

A second way to use the phone book is to look in the yellow pages. The following is a partial list of headings that you might look under in searching for help.

Abuse
Adoptions
Birth Control Information
Child Abuse
Child Protective Services
Children and Family Services
Churches
Clergy
Clinics

Counseling
Crisis Intervention Services
Disabled Services
Family Planning
General Information and Referral
Health
Legal
Marriage Counselors
Mental Health Services
Psychiatrists
Psychologists
Rape
Sexual Assault
Sexually Transmitted Diseases
Social Service Organizations
Venereal Disease

Some yellow pages offer an index in the back, where you can look up the specific service that you want. Remember, if you call any organization and it does not offer the service that you require, ask for suggestions about where you might try next. Most helping agencies are very aware of what resources may be available in your vicinity.

Again, do not hesitate to ask the qualifications of any professional counselor you are considering, prior to setting up an appointment. And if at any point you do not feel that you are getting the help you need, shop around for another resource. That is your right as a consumer.

Organizations

Here is a list of national organizations that might be helpful in answering any questions you have and in referring you to an agency in your area that can be of assistance.

Abortion and Birth Alternatives

Florence Crittenton Association
440 1st Street N.W., Suite 310, Washington, D.C. 20001
(202) 638-2952

A counseling and referral organization with many affiliates, which explores alternatives to abortion.

National Abortion Federation Hot Line
(800) 772-9100

Toll-free referral and information services.

National Abortion Rights Action League
1424 K Street, N.W., Washington, DC 20005

A national organization that favors abortion as an alternative.

National Right to Life Committee
419 7th Street, N.W., Washington, DC 20045

A national organization that opposes abortion as an alternative.

AIDS

National AIDS Hot Line
(800) 342-2437

A toll-free national hot line provided by the Public Health Service, which provides recorded information and additional phone numbers for people wanting a referral or more information about AIDS.

Child Sexual Abuse

Parents United, Inc.
P.O. Box 952, San Jose, CA 95108
(408) 280-5055

An organization that provides counseling for the whole family of sexually abused children.

Counseling and Referrals

Family Service Association of America
11700 West Lake Park Drive, Milwaukee, WI 53224
(414) 359-2111

A general counseling service with affiliated agencies throughout the United States.

Planned Parenthood Federation of America, Inc.
810 Seventh Avenue, New York, NY 10019
(212) 541-7800

A national organization that offers medical, educational, counseling, and referral services for many aspects of sexuality, including birth control and sexually transmitted diseases. It has hundreds of affiliates throughout the country.

Disabilities

Coalition on Sexuality and Disability, Inc.
841 Broadway, Suite 205, New York, NY 10003
(212) 242-3900

An association that provides medical information, educational services, and counseling for people with disabilities.

Family Planning (See also "Counseling and Referrals")

Zero Population Growth
1400 16th St. N.W., Suite 320, Washington, DC 20036
(202) 332-2200

Provides educational materials that emphasize how personal life-styles can affect the quality of life for future generations.

Gay Services

Gay Community Services Center
1213 North Highland, Hollywood, CA 90028
(213) 464-7400

A center that provides psychological, medical, vocational, legal, and youth counseling services.

Gay Switchboard
(215) 546-7100

A Philadelphia-based hot line providing information and referral services nationwide.

Gayellow Pages
Box 292, Village Station, New York, NY 10014

A directory of gay services, organizations, and businesses.

Parents and Friends of Lesbians and Gays (Parents FLAG)
P.O. Box 27605, Washington, D.C. 20038
(202) 638-4200

A national organization that provides support and counseling for parents and friends of gays.

Hot Lines

Sex Information Help Line
(213) 653-1123

A Los Angeles-based hot line that provides information and referrals nationwide.

Sex Education and Therapy

American Association of Sex Educators, Counselors, and
 Therapists (AASECT)

11 Dupont Circle N.W., Suite 220, Washington, DC 20036
(202) 462-1171

*A national professional organization of sex therapists and
sex educators with members throughout the United States.*

Sex Information and Education Council of the United States
(SIECUS)
32 Washington Pl., Room 52, New York, NY 10003
(212) 673-3850

*A national organization that offers information about sex-
uality. It provides a recommended reading list on request
and puts out its own publications dealing with sexual information and issues.*

Sexually Transmitted Diseases
See also under AIDS.

The Herpes Resource Center
260 Sheridan Avenue, Palo Alto, CA 94306
(415) 328-7710

*A comprehensive resource center that provides a newsletter
with up-to-date information, counseling, and referral services in regard to herpes.*

VD National Hotline
(800) 227-8922

A toll-free counseling and referral service.

Single Parenting
Parents Without Partners
P.O. Box 700, Clinton, MD 20795
(202) 638-1320

A nonsectarian organization for single men and women with chapters throughout the world. Publishes a monthly magazine, The Single Parent.

Transsexuality

J.T.C.P.
P.O. Box 184, San Juan Capistrano, CA 92693
(714) 496-5227

An information and referral service for those seeking information about transsexuality.

GLOSSARY

Some of the terms defined in this glossary are not contained in this book. They are included because they are words that your teenager may hear or read from other sources and may ask for more information about.

Abortion—The ending of a pregnancy prematurely. The egg, the embryo, or the fetus (depending upon the stage of pregnancy) is removed or expelled from the uterus.

Acne—Large, deep pimples and blackheads, which are common during adolescence.

Acquaintance rape—Sexual relations forced upon a person by someone he or she knows. It is a form of sexual assault.

Adolescence—The period in a young person's life beginning with puberty and ending with adulthood.

Adoption—The process in which a child is legally made a part of a family into which he or she was not born.

Afterbirth—The material made up of the placenta and fetal sacs, which are typically expelled after the fetus has been delivered.

AIDS (Acquired Immune Deficiency Syndrome)—A condition caused by a virus in which the body's immune system no longer works effectively. It can leave the person susceptible to many deadly forms of infection and disease. Gay and bisexual men have been especially vulnerable to catching AIDS.

Amnion—A sac containing fluid which encloses and protects the fetus within the uterus.

Anal sex (anal intercourse)—A form of sexual intercourse in which the penis is inserted into the partner's rectum.

Anorexia—A condition characterized by a severe lack of appetite and inability to eat, usually caused by psychological problems.

Anus—The opening of the body leading from the rectum, from which feces are expelled from the body.

Birth control pill—A pill taken to ensure that sexual intercourse does not result in pregnancy. Birth control pills are made from artificial hormones.

Bisexual—A person who feels attracted to both males and females and engages in sexual activity with both sexes.

Calendar method—See Rhythm method

Candidiasis—Often called a yeast infection, it is an overgrowth of yeast fungus in the vagina, which causes irritation.

Catheter—A hollow tube used to drain fluids from the body. Often used to drain urine from the bladder when normal urination is physically impeded.

Cervical cap—A contraceptive device that forms a caplike barrier over the cervix, preventing sperm from entering.

Cervix—The narrow, necklike portion at the bottom of the uterus, which extends into the vagina.

Cesarean section (C-section)—A childbirth procedure in which the child is delivered through incisions made in the abdomen and uterus.

Chancre—A painless sore, characteristic of the early stages of syphilis. The secretions from the chancre are highly contagious.

Child molestation—See Sexual molestation

Chlamydia—A sexually transmitted disease caused by a bacterialike organism. Its symptoms resemble gonorrhea.

Circumcision—The process in which the foreskin is surgically removed from around the top of the penis.

Clitoral hood—Tissue from the labia minora that forms a hoodlike covering over the clitoris.

Clitoris—A small, extremely sensitive female sex organ located immediately in front of the urethra. Stimulation of the clitoris is often involved in a woman reaching orgasm.

Coitus—A medical term for sexual intercourse.

Coitus interruptus—A very ineffective means of birth control in which the penis is withdrawn from the vagina prior to ejaculation.

Combination pill—A type of birth control pill that contains both estrogen and progestin.

Coming Out—The making public of a person's homosexuality.

Conception—The joining of the male sperm and the female ovum to form a fertilized egg.

Condom—Commonly called a "rubber," or prophylactic. A baglike rubber or membrane covering worn on the penis both as a contraceptive device and as a way of protecting against the spread of sexually transmitted diseases.

Contraceptive—Any device used to minimize the possibility of pregnancy as a result of sexual intercourse.

Contraceptive foam—A form of birth control that consists of sperm-killing chemical agents contained in a foamy base. It is inserted into the vagina prior to intercourse.

Contraceptive sponge—A form of birth control that consists of a soft plastic sponge containing a spermicide, which is placed over the cervix.

Cowper's glands—Two small glands that connect with the urethra in a male, just below the prostate gland. They emit a bit of fluid before ejaculation, which can contain sperm.

Cross-dresser—Also called a transvestite. A person, usually male, who has a strong compulsion to dress in the clothing of the opposite sex.

Cunnilingus—The stimulation of the female vulva by the mouth.

D and C (dilation and curettage)—A medical procedure in which the cervix is dilated and then the lining and contents of the uterus are scraped away with a metal instrument. Infrequently, this procedure is used as a method of abortion.

D and E (dilation and evacuation)—A medical procedure commonly used for abortions during the thirteenth to sixteenth week of pregnancy. In this procedure, the cervix is dilated and the contents of the uterus are eliminated through a combination of scraping and suction.

Date rape—Sexual relations forced upon a person by his or her date. It is a form of sexual assault.

DES (Diethylstilbestrol)—A synthetic estrogen that has been linked to potential cancer risks in women and their children. Used by pregnant women in the 1940s and 1950s to prevent miscarriages, the drug is no longer prescribed by doctors for this purpose. However, a small amount of DES is contained in some morning-after pills.

Diaphragm—A contraceptive device made of soft latex, which acts as a cup covering the female's cervix. It should be used in combination with a spermicide.

Douche—The process in which the vagina is flushed out with a liquid.

Ducts—Tubelike structures in the body that conduct fluids or secretions.

Dyspareunia—Painful intercourse.

Ectopic pregnancy—A pregnancy in which the fertilized egg implants in a location other than the uterus. Typically, the alternate location is one of the fallopian tubes. This is also called a tubal pregnancy.

Egg—Another term for an ovum.

Ejaculation—The sudden shooting out of semen from the penis, which almost always occurs when a male experiences orgasm.

Embryo—The stage of development of an unborn infant from conception through eight weeks.

Epididymis—A long, compactly wound tube in which the newly developed sperm mature inside the scrotum.

Erection—The enlarging and stiffening of the penis as a result of an increased blood flow to that area. Erections are usually attributed to sexual stimulation, but other factors can cause them.

Estrogen—A hormone that produces female sex characteristics. Estrogens also affect the female's menstrual cycle. "Combination" birth control pills contain synthetic estrogens.

Fallopian tubes—The tubes that transport the eggs from each ovary to the uterus. Conception usually takes place in these tubes.

Fertile—Capable of becoming pregnant.

Fertilization—See Conception

Fetus—The developing infant inside the mother, from the eighth week of pregnancy until birth. Before the eighth week it is referred to as an embryo.

Forceps—A surgical tonglike instrument that is sometimes used during the delivery of a child to help pull the child through the birth canal.

Foreplay—The beginning stages of sexual play prior to sexual intercourse.

Foreskin—The fold of skin that covers the tip of a boy's penis at birth. Often it is removed by circumcision.

Foster care—The process in which a family is given temporary custody of a child because his needs cannot be met by his own family. In most states foster parents must be approved by a state agency.

Gay—A popularly used term for anything having to do with homosexuality.

Gender—The definition of a person's sex as male or female.

Gender identity—A person's own conviction of maleness or femaleness.

Geneticist—An expert in the science of genetics.

Genital herpes—A sexually transmitted disease whose primary symptoms include blisters and sores around the genital area. Outbreaks can reoccur repeatedly, and, as yet, there is no cure.

Genitals—The external sex organs of both males and females.

Gland—Any organ of the body that produces a secretion.

Glans—The head of the penis.

Gonorrhea—A common sexually transmitted disease caused by a bacterial infection. Although dangerous, it often produces no early symptoms in females.

Growth spurt—The period during adolescence when the body increases in size relatively rapidly.

Gynecomastia—A temporary enlarging of the breasts in males. This occurs in about 80 percent of teenage boys going through puberty.

HCG (human chorionic gonadotrophin)—The female hormone that is measured in order to confirm whether a woman is pregnant. It is produced by the developing embryo or placenta during pregnancy.

Health care practitioner—A physician, nurse, or other person qualified and legally authorized to provide certain types of medical care.

Hepatitis—An infection of the liver, which is sometimes transmitted sexually.

Herpes—See Genital herpes

Heterosexual—A person whose sole or primary sexual attraction is to people of the opposite sex.

Homosexual—A person whose sole or primary sexual attraction is to people of the same sex.

Hormones—Chemical messengers produced by the endocrine glands. They regulate many of the body's activities, including sexual functioning and maturation.

Hygiene—The science of health and practices that promote health.

Hymen—The membrane that covers the entrance to the vagina.

Impotence—A condition in which a male is unable to attain an erection sufficient to engage in sexual intercourse.

Incest—Sexual activity between close relatives.

Infertile—Not capable of becoming pregnant.

IUD (intrauterine device)—A contraceptive device made of metal or plastic, which is inserted by a physician into a woman's uterus. It is not recommended for teenagers.

Labia—The lips of the female genital area. There are two sets of lips. The labia majora are the larger, outer lips, and the labia minora are the smaller, inner lips. Both are part of the vulva.

Labor—The process of giving birth to a child.

Lateral position—A position of intercourse in which the couple lies in a side-by-side position, facing each other.

Lesbian—A female homosexual.

Male superior position (missionary position)—A position of intercourse in which the male lies on top, facing the female.

Mammary glands—Milk-producing glands contained within the female breasts.

Masturbation—Self-pleasuring by touching one's own genitals to produce sexual excitement and often orgasm.

Menarche—The onset of menstruation in a young woman.

Menopause—The time of life when a woman ceases to menstruate. This will usually occur between the ages of forty-five and fifty-five.

Menstrual cycle—A woman's fertility cycle. Most commonly, this cycle is between twenty-eight and thirty days, but it can vary considerably from woman to woman and in the same woman.

Menstrual sponges—Special sponges inserted into the vagina like tampons (see Tampons) in order to catch the menstrual flow before it leaves the body. These sponges have not yet been approved by the federal government because their safety has not been sufficiently proven.

Menstruation—The part of the menstrual cycle in which the inner lining of the uterus, along with a small amount of blood, is eliminated through the vagina. Often referred to as a period.

Minipill—A type of birth control pill that contains only a small dose of synthetic progestin rather than both progestin and estrogen as contained in combination pills.

Mittelschmerz—A term meaning "middle pain" in German, it refers to the cramping or slight abdominal pain produced when the egg breaks loose and the ovary bleeds a little during ovulation.

Mons pubis—The "pubic mound." The soft mound of tissue located just above a female's external genitals and covering the pubic bone.

Morning-after pill—Birth control pills taken the morning after unprotected intercourse, which reduce the chances of becoming pregnant.

Morning sickness—Nausea that is rather typical in women during the early stages of pregnancy and most common in the morning hours.

Mucus—Liquid secretions from the various moist membranes in the body, such as the nose, vagina, and cervix.

Mucus method—A fertility-awareness method in which one

learns to recognize changes in cervical mucus at different stages of the menstrual cycle.

Natural methods—Methods of birth control that are based upon trying to predict when a female is fertile. None of these methods is recommended for adolescents.

Nipple—The tip of the breast, from which milk is ejected when a woman is nursing.

Nocturnal emission—Ejaculation of semen during a male's sleep. Often referred to as a "wet dream."

Nonoxynol-9—An ingredient of most contraceptive foams. It is believed to have some positive effect in protecting against contracting AIDS.

Nursing—The feeding of a child at the mother's breast.

Oral contraceptive—See Birth control pill

Oral sex (oral-genital sex)—Any sexual activity that involves contact between the mouth and the genitals.

Orgasm—The peak experience that occurs at the height of sexual excitement, resulting in reflex contractions of the muscles in the pelvic region and a discharge of sexual tension. Often referred to as "coming" or climax.

Ovaries—A pair of sex glands in the female that are responsible for the production of ova (eggs). In addition, they produce female sex hormones. They are located on each side of the upper portion of the uterus.

Ovulation—The process, which occurs approximately once each month, of the ovum breaking through the wall of the ovary in order to begin its journey down the fallopian tube.

Ovum (plural, ova)—The egg released by the female's ovary. It is the female reproductive cell.

Pap smear—A test in which cells from the cervix are examined for the presence of abnormalities, in order to detect signs of cancer of the cervix.

Pelvic exam—A medical exam of the female genitals and internal reproductive organs.

Pelvic inflammatory disease (PID)—An inflammation of

the fallopian tubes, which may also involve the uterus and the pelvic cavity. It is very dangerous and can lead to sterility.

Penis—The cylindrical male organ used for urination and for sexual activities such as intercourse.

Period—See Menstruation

Petting—Touching by a partner of any of the sensitive sexual areas of the body.

Placenta—An organ that exchanges oxygen, nutrients, and waste material between the mother and the fetus. It is attached to the inside wall of the uterus.

Pregnancy—The time between conception and childbirth when the embryo or fetus is developing in the uterus.

Premature ejaculation—A sexual difficulty in men, in which ejaculation occurs too quickly, thus making sexual satisfaction difficult for one or both partners.

Premenstrual syndrome (PMS)—Physical and emotional discomfort that some women experience during the days before menstruation.

Progesterone—One of the female sex hormones. Progesterone causes the lining of the uterus to prepare for implantation of a fertilized egg and helps support the embryo or fetus within the uterus during pregnancy. It is also contained in birth control pills.

Progestin—A synthetic form of progesterone.

Prostate gland—A gland in the male that surrounds the urethra, just below the bladder. This gland is responsible for producing much of the seminal fluid.

Prosthesis (penile)—A permanent implant, surgically placed into the penis of men who are impotent, which enables them to get an erection.

Psychiatrist—A mental health professional whose primary training is in the area of medicine.

Psychologist—A mental health professional whose primary

training is in the area of the psychological aspects of behavior.

Puberty—The period during which a boy or girl matures physically and becomes capable of reproduction.

Pubic area—The area of the body just above the external genitals. It becomes covered with hair during puberty.

Pubic bone—The front bone in the group of bones that form the pelvic girdle.

Pubic hair—The hair that covers the area above the vagina in females and penis in males. Pubic hair is one of the first signs of the onset of puberty.

Pubic lice—Small, crab-shaped parasites that can be spread by sexual contact.

Rape—Forced sexual intercourse. It is one form of sexual assault.

Refractory period—The period after orgasm in most men, during which they are incapable of having another erection or ejaculation. This period may last from a few minutes to a few days, depending upon such factors as age, health, and degree of sexual excitement.

Rhythm method—A method of birth control in which sexual intercourse is planned to coincide with times when it is thought that fertilization of the female's egg is unlikely. This tends to be an extremely unreliable form of birth control, especially for teenagers.

Role model—A person whose behavior is used as an example to guide another person's conduct.

"Rubber"—A slang term for a condom.

Sanitary napkins—Strips of absorbent material used to collect the menstrual fluid during a female's period.

Scrotum—The pouch of skin in a male that contains the two testes.

Self-esteem—The sense of value with which a person regards himself or herself.

Semen—A thick, sticky, whitish liquid that spurts from the penis during ejaculation. It ordinarily includes a mixture of sperm and seminal fluid.

Seminal vesicles—Two sacklike structures in the male body that produce a secretion that begins the whipping motion of the sperms' tails.

Sex glands—Glands of the endocrine system that produce sex hormones. The male sex glands are the testes, and the female sex glands are the ovaries.

Sexual assault—Sexual relations forced upon a person against his or her will. Sexual assault often involves physical force or violence but also includes sex forced by the use of threats.

Sexual harassment—Any unwanted attention of a sexual nature that creates discomfort or interferes with work or school performance.

Sexual intercourse—The placement of the male's penis into the female's vagina.

Sexual molestation—Sexual acts that are forced upon a child by an adult, whether the child consents to them or not. Also referred to as child molestation.

Sexually transmitted diseases (STDs)—Formerly called venereal diseases. Any of a number of diseases that can be transmitted during the close body contact that occurs with sexual activity. Gonorrhea, herpes, and syphilis are some examples.

Shaft—The longer part (or body) of the clitoris or penis.

Smegma—A cheeselike mixture of secretions and skin cells that can build up under the foreskin of the uncircumcised penis or around the lips of the vulva.

Speculum—A duck-billed medical instrument used to open and view the vagina during a pelvic exam.

Sperm—Microscopic cells that are responsible for fertilizing the female egg (ovum). These reproductive cells are produced by the testes.

Spermicide—A substance used for birth control that, when placed in the female's vagina, kills sperm before they can meet with ovum. These substances may be in the form of foams, jellies, creams, suppositories, or, in a relatively new method, a special sponge. Spermicides are often used along with a condom or a diaphragm for greater effectiveness.

Statutory rape—The legal term for sexual intercourse with any adolescent under the age of consent. Often these laws apply only to females under the age of consent. It does not matter whether the intercourse was voluntary on the teenager's part.

STD—See Sexually transmitted diseases

Sterility—Inability to become pregnant or to impregnate.

Sterilization—Any medical procedure that makes a person permanently unable to produce offspring. Common methods of sterilization are vasectomy in the male and tubal ligation in the female. It is not ordinarily recommended as a form of birth control for teenagers.

Syphilis—A highly contagious sexually transmitted disease. One of the common symptoms during the early stages are chancres, which disappear as the disease enters the more dangerous later stages.

Tampons—Absorbent material that is inserted into the vagina during a female's period to catch the menstrual flow before it leaves the body.

Testes—The two male sex glands located in the scrotum. They produce sperm and male sex hormones. Often referred to in slang as "balls" or "nuts."

Testicles—Another name for the testes.

Testosterone—The primary male sex hormone.

Toxic shock syndrome (TSS)—A dangerous disease caused by a bacterial infection, most often occurring in menstruating women. It may be related to the use of tampons.

Transsexual—A person who is biologically of one gender,

but constantly feels that he or she is meant to be the other. Surgical procedures to change the person's sex may be performed.

Transvestite—See Cross-dresser

Trichomoniasis—An irritation or infection of the female genitals caused by a microscopic one-celled animal. Males also contract and transmit "trich," but seldom have symptoms of the disease.

Trimester—A three-month segment of pregnancy. Pregnancy is typically divided into three trimesters.

Tubal ligation—The most common method of surgical sterilization performed on females, in which the fallopian tubes are cut so the ova cannot meet the sperm.

Tubal pregnancy—See Ectopic pregnancy

Umbilical cord—The cord connecting the fetus with the placenta.

Urethra—The tube through which urine is discharged from the body. In the male it is also used to ejaculate the semen.

Uterus—The womb. The organ that holds the growing baby during pregnancy.

Vacuum aspiration—A method of abortion typically used in the first three months of pregnancy in which the contents of the uterus are removed with a vacuum.

Vagina—The passage that connects the uterus with the vulva. During sexual intercourse, the erect penis is placed into the vagina. During childbirth, the vagina acts as the birth canal through which the newborn child is delivered.

Vaginismus—A sexual dysfunction in females in which the muscles surrounding the vagina involuntarily go into spasm when penetration is attempted.

Vaginitis—Any infection or irritation of the vagina.

Vas deferens—A duct consisting of two narrow tubes that carry sperm in the male from the testes to the urethra.

Vasectomy—A common method of surgical sterilization

performed on males, in which the vas deferens is cut. After a vasectomy, the male still ejaculates the seminal fluid, but without the sperm, which are necessary for reproduction.

VCF (Vaginal contraceptive film)—A new contraceptive product consisting of paper-thin, two-inch-square films containing spermicide, which are inserted into the vagina prior to intercourse.

VD—See Sexually transmitted diseases

Venereal disease—See Sexually transmitted diseases

Venereal warts—Small bumps on or near the genitals, caused by a virus, which can be spread by sexual contact.

Vestibule—The indented area of the female vulva between the inner lips. It contains the openings of the vagina and the urethra.

Virgin—A person who has never engaged in sexual intercourse.

Vulva—A woman's external sex organs.

Wet dream—An ejaculation that occurs during a male's sleep. It is also referred to as a nocturnal emission.

Withdrawal—See Coitus interruptus

Yeast infection—Another term for candidiasis

Zygote—The single cell that results from the union of an egg and sperm after fertilization.

NOTES

1. Your Child Will Receive a Sex Education

1. Centers for Disease Control, Division of Venereal Disease Control, 1988.
2. Alan Guttmacher Institute, "Research Note: Unintended Pregnancy among American Women," *Family Planning Perspective* 19, no. 2 (March-April 1987), 77.
3. AIDS Weekly Surveillance Report, AIDS Program, Centers for Infectious Diseases, Atlanta, October 17, 1988.
4. The Alan Guttmacher Institute, "School Based Health Program Helps Inner-City Teens Delay Sex and Prevent Pregnancy," News Release, July 9, 1986.
5. J. Dryfoos, "What the United States Can Learn about Prevention of Teenage Pregnancy from Other Developed Countries," *SIECUS Report* 14, no. 2 (November 1985), 1–7.
6. S. R. Edwards, "Adolescent Boys and Sex: Irresponsible or Neglected?" *SIECUS Report* 15, no. 4 (March 1987), 1–4.
7. R. E. Lovett, "An Expert Tries to Explain to His Son

the Facts of, er, Life," *Los Angeles Times*, Sept. 4, 1984, part 2, pp. 5, 20.
8. A. Hass, *Teenage Sexuality* (New York: Pinnacle Books, 1981), 58.
9. Ibid., 56.
10. R. Coles and G. Stokes, *Sex and the American Teenager* (New York: Rolling Stone Press, 1985), 73.

2. Finding a Beginning Point

1. J. M. Tanner, *Growth at Adolescence*, 2nd ed. (Oxford: Blackwell, 1962).
2. A. Hass, *Teenage Sexuality* (New York: Pinnacle Books, 1981), 207.
3. Ibid., 209.

3. Understanding the Obstacles

1. B. Cosby, *Fatherhood* (New York: Berkley Books, 1987), 91.
2. H. G. Ginott, *Between Parent and Teenager* (New York: Avon Books, 1971), 13.
3. C. Crowe, *Fast Times at Ridgemont High: A True Story* (New York: Simon and Schuster, 1981), 66.
4. Ibid.
5. A. Hass, *Teenage Sexuality* (New York: Pinnacle Books, 1981), 197.
6. Ibid., 197.
7. Ibid., 199.

4. Methods of Sex Education

1. J. Voss and J. Gale, *A Young Woman's Guide to Sex* (New York: Henry Holt, 1986), 6.

6. A Quick Primer on Communicating with Your Teenager

1. A. Hass, *Teenage Sexuality* (New York: Pinnacle Books, 1981), 210.

9. Touching and Sexual Intimacy

1. A. Hass, *Teenage Sexuality* (New York: Pinnacle Books, 1981), 100.
2. Bernie Zilbergeld, *Male Sexuality* (Boston: Little Brown, 1978), 135.
3. C. Cassell, *Straight from the Heart* (New York: Simon and Schuster, 1987), 104.

10. Conception and Contraception

1. Swedish Television Corporation, *The Miracle of Life* [videorecording] (New York: Crown Video, 1986).
2. R. Coles and G. Stokes, *Sex and the American Teenager* (New York: Rolling Stone Press, 1985), 121.

13. Homosexuality: The Fears and the Realities

1. J. Gale, *A Young Man's Guide to Sex* (New York: Holt Rinehart, 1984), 129–30.
2. Ibid., 162–63.
3. A. C. Kinsey, W. B. Pomeroy, and C. E. Martin, *Sexual Behavior in the Human Male* (Philadelphia: Saunders, 1948), and A. C. Kinsey, W. B. Pomeroy, C. E. Martin, and P. Gebhard, *Sexual Behavior in the Human Female* (Philadelphia: Saunders, 1953).

14. Preventing Sexual Exploitation

1. R. Coles and G. Stokes, *Sex and the American Teenager* (New York: Rolling Stone Press, 1985), 109.
2. J. Voss and J. Gale, *A Young Woman's Guide to Sex* (New York: Henry Holt, 1986), 235.
3. Ibid., 237–38.
4. Crime Prevention Center, California Department of Justice, *Sexual Assault Prevention Handbook* (Sacramento, 1982). Write: Office of the Attorney General, 555 Capitol Mall, Suite 290, Sacramento, CA 95814.

15. The Sexually Active Teenager

1. R. Coles and G. Stokes, *Sex and the American Teenager* (New York: Rolling Stone Press, 1985), 94.

16. Pregnancy

1. Sex Information and Education Council of the United States, *Teenage Pregnancy*, 6.

17. Dealing with Sexual Trauma

1. Ms. Magazine Campus Project on Sexual Assault, funded by the National Center for the Prevention and Control of Rape, in *Ms.*, October 1985, 56.
2. R. Coles and G. Stokes, *Sex and the American Teenager* (New York: Rolling Stone Press, 1985), 108.
3. S. Forward and C. Buck, *Betrayal of Innocence* (New York: Penguin Books, 1987), 85.
4. Superior Court Transcript, San Jose, CA Juvenile Di-

vision, September 2, 1969.
5. S. Forward and C. Buck, *Betrayal of Innocence*, 19.

18. If You're a Single Parent

1. R. Coles and G. Stokes, *Sex and the American Teenager* (New York: Rolling Stone Press, 1985), 77, 144.

19. The Homosexual Teenager

1. W. V. Pawlowski, "Growing Up Gay: Lessons in Becoming Invisible," *Family Life Educator* 3, no. 2 (Winter 1984), 25–26.
2. F. Hanckel and J. Cunningham, *A Way of Love, a Way of Life: A Young Person's Introduction to What It Means to be Gay* (New York: Lothrop, Lee and Shephard, 1979), 80–81.

20. The Handicapped Teenager

1. B. H. H. Dechesne, C. Pons, and A. M. C. M. Schellen, eds., *Sexuality and Handicap: Problems of Motor Handicapped People* (New York: Charles C. Thomas, 1986), 131.
2. S. Cole, *Women and Sex Therapy: Closing the Circle of Sexual Knowledge* (New York: Harrington Park Press, 1988).
3. T. Mooney, T. M. Cole, and R. Chilgren, *Sexual Options for Paraplegics and Quadriplegics* (Boston: Little Brown, 1975).
4. S. Gordon and J. Gordon, *Raising a Child Conservatively in a Sexually Permissive World* (New York: Simon and Schuster, 1983), 190.

Afterword

1. W. H. Masters and V. Johnson, "Teaching Your Children About Sex," *Redbook*, September 1975.

BIBLIOGRAPHY

The following is a list of books and other materials that might be useful for expanding on the information presented in this volume. The entries are listed according to topic.

Abortion

Corsaro, M., and C. Korzeniowsky. *A Woman's Guide to Safe Abortion*. New York: Holt, Rinehart and Winston, 1983.

A realistic approach to the planning of an abortion. Also includes information on how to avoid future unwanted pregnancies.

Assertiveness Training

Butler, P. *Self-Assertion for Women*. New York: Harper and Row, 1981.

The Biology of Sex

Swedish Television Corporation. *The Miracle of Life* [videorecording]. New York: Crown Video, 1986.

An outstanding video that shows the biological intricacies of what occurs inside the human body during and after a sexual experience. It is fascinating viewing for parents and teens.

The Disabled and Sex

Ayrault, E. W. *Sex, Love, and the Physically Handicapped.* New York: Continuum, 1981.

Johnson, W. R., and W. Kempton. *Sex Education Counseling of Special Groups: The Mentally and Physically Handicapped, Ill and Elderly.* 2nd edition. Springfield, Ill.: Charles C. Thomas, 1980.

Mooney, T. O., T. M. Cole, and R. A. Chilgren. *Sexual Options for Paraplegics and Quadriplegics.* Boston: Little Brown, 1975.
An excellent source for helping the disabled person reach his or her maximum sexual potential.

Fiction

Blume, J. *Forever.* Scarsdale, N.Y.: Bradbury Press, 1975.
A novel written for teenagers that gives a realistic view of teenage sexuality.

Health

Boston Women's Health Collective. *The New Our Bodies, Ourselves.* New York: Simon and Schuster, 1984.
A health-oriented book on women's bodies and concerns written by women.

Homosexuality

Fairchild, B., and N. Howard. *Now That You Know: What Every Parent Should Know about Homosexuality.* New York: Harcourt Brace Jovanovich, 1979.

A book helpful for parents trying to understand their homosexual child.

Hanckel, F., and J. Cunningham. *A Way of Love, a Way of Life: A Young Person's Introduction to What It Means to Be Gay.* New York: Lothrop, Lee and Shepard, 1979.

A sensitively written book for the teenager trying to understand what it means to be gay.

Jones, C. *Understanding Gay Relatives and Friends.* New York: Seabury Press, 1987.

A very personal book to help the relatives and friends of homosexuals.

Silverstein, C. *A Family Matter: A Parent's Guide to Homosexuality.* New York: McGraw-Hill, 1977.

A book to help parents of homosexuals deal with their concerns.

Legal Rights

Sussman, A. *The Rights of Young People.* New York: Avon Books, 1977.

A guide for young people about legal rights. Covers several areas of sexuality, such as marriage, contraception, and abortion.

Male Sexuality

Hite, S. *The Hite Report on Male Sexuality.* New York: Alfred A. Knopf, 1981.

Results of a survey of more than 7,000 men, listing and discussing some of the common (and uncommon) fears and sexual preferences of males.

Zilbergeld, B. *Male Sexuality*. Boston: Little, Brown, 1978.
A well-written, easily readable book for the man or woman trying to gain a more complete understanding of the physiology and the emotional side of male sexuality.

For Men

Wagenvoord, J., and P. Bailey, eds. *Women: A Book for Men*. New York: Avon Books, 1979.
A helpful book for men trying to broaden their understanding of women.

Parenting

Ginott, H. G. *Between Parent and Teenager*. New York: Avon Books, 1971.

Pogrebin, L. C. *Growing Up Free: Raising Your Child in the '80s*. New York: McGraw-Hill, 1980.

Pregnancy

Gordon, S., and M. Wollin. *Parenting: A Guide for Young People*. New York: William H. Sadlier, 1975.
Written for the young person preparing to become a parent.

Oettinger, K. B., with E. C. Mooney. *Not My Daughter: Facing Up to Adolescent Pregnancy*. New York: St. Martin's Press, 1980.
Written for the parents of a pregnant teenager.

Rape, Sexual Assault, and Sexual Exploitation

Adams, C., and J. Fay. "Nobody Told Me It Was Rape." *A Parent's Guide for Talking with Teenagers about*

Acquaintance Rape and Sexual Exploitation. Santa Cruz: Network Publications, 1984.

Bateman, P. *Acquaintance Rape: Awareness and Prevention.* Write: Alternatives to Fear, 1605 17th Avenue, Seattle, WA 98122.
A workbook for teenagers on preventing and coping with acquaintance rape.

Fay, J., and B. J. Flerchinger. *Top Secret: Sexual Assault Information for Teenagers Only.* King County Rape Relief, 1982. Write: King County Rape Relief, 304 S. 43rd, Renton, WA 98055.

Crime Prevention Center, California Department of Justice. *Sexual Assault Prevention Handbook.* Write: Office of the Attorney General, 555 Capitol Mall, Suite 290, Sacramento, CA 95814.

Ledray, L. *Recovering from Rape.* New York: Henry Holt, 1986.
A comprehensive handbook for survivors of sexual assault and for their families, lovers, and friends.

Religion

Gordis, R. *Love and Sex: A Modern Jewish Perspective.* New York: Farrar, Straus and Giroux, 1978.

Koznik, A., et al. *Human Sexuality: New Directions in American Catholic Thought.* New York: Paulist Press, 1977.

Taylor, J. J., ed. *Sex: Thoughts for Contemporary Christians.* New York: Doubleday, 1972.

Reproduction

Demarest, Robert J., and John J. Sciarra. *Conception, Birth and Contraception: A Visual Presentation*. New York: McGraw-Hill, 1976.

A well-illustrated book for the middle-to-later teen about the process of human reproduction.

Sexually Transmitted Diseases

Corsaro, M., and C. Korzeniowsky. *STD: A Commonsense Guide to Sexually Transmitted Diseases*. New York: Holt, Rinehart and Winston, 1982.

A nonjudgmental, straightforward book for those interested in recognizing and understanding sexually transmitted diseases.

Gordon, S. *Facts about VD for Today's Youth*. Revised edition. Fayetteville, N.Y.: Ed-U Press, 1979.

Information about sexually transmitted diseases; stresses the importance of prevention and early treatment.

For Teens—General

Gordon, S., and R. Conant. *You! The Teenage Survival Book*. 2nd edition. New York: Times Books, 1984.

A personal book about sexuality and teenage concerns.

Hass, A., Ph.D. *Teenage Sexuality*. New York: Pinnacle Books, 1981.

Results of a survey in which teenagers discuss their attitudes about and their expectations of sex.

For Teens and Preteens/Male

Gale, J. *A Young Man's Guide to Sex.* New York: Holt, Rinehart and Winston, 1984.

A sensitively written, easily readable book for an adolescent or young adult male trying to gain an understanding about the facts and emotions involved in becoming a sexual person. Paperback version available.

For Teens and Preteens/Female

Gardner-Loulan, J., B. Loppez, and M. Quackenbush. *Period.* San Francisco: New Glide Publications, 1979.

A book for preteens that explains in an understanding and supportive way what menstruation is all about. Well illustrated.

Voss, J., and J. Gale. *A Young Woman's Guide to Sex.* New York: Henry Holt, 1984.

A sensitively written, easily readable book for an adolescent or young adult female trying to gain an understanding about the facts and emotions involved in becoming a sexual person. Paperback version available.

INDEX

Abortion, 3–4, 59
  choice of, 137–38, 142, 144–46
  incidence of, among teenagers, 5
  legal aspects of, 145–46
  medical procedures in, 145–46
  morality of, 6–7
  organizational resources and, 19
  reading matter on, 223
  sex education and, 9
  teenagers' fears about, 144
"Absolutes," avoiding use of, 51
Acne, 64–65
Acquaintance rape, 71, 121–23
Adoption, 144, 148–49
Advertising, 3, 34, 57
Africa, 99
Age
  masturbation and, 68–69
  of puberty, 18–19, 61, 66
  readiness for information and, 12, 18–20
  sexual experience and, 12
AIDS (Acquired Immune Deficiency Syndrome), 3, 12, 33, 49, 55, 59, 70, 95–104, 109, 171
  contraceptives and, 76, 81–83, 96, 98, 100–101
  high-risk activities, 97, 100
  high-risk partners, 99
  homosexuality and, 96, 97, 171, 173
  incidence of, 6
  key facts about, 95–97
  organizational help and, 197
  other STDs (sexually transmitted diseases) and, 102–3
  precautions against, 98–101
  teenagers as at-risk group for, 6, 59, 96
Alan Guttmacher Institute, 4
Alcohol use
  forced sex and, 123
  by handicapped, 179, 189
  sexual activity and, 101
American Association of Sex Educators, Counselors, and Therapists (AASECT), 199

233

Anal intercourse, AIDS and, 97, 100
Anorexia, 61
Artificial insemination, 75, 188
Assertiveness training, 223

Baby oil, condoms and, 81
Birth control. *See* Contraception
Birth control pills, 76, 87–89
  side effects of, 88–89
Bisexuals, 99
Blackheads, 64
Blastocyst, 76
Blood in AIDS transmission, 96, 97, 99
Books, 223–29
  to build self-esteem, 56
  in sex education, 29–32, 40, 62
  and sexual coercion, 70
Boredom in handicapped, 178, 186
Boys vs. girls. *See* Gender differences
Braces, handicapped and, 179
Breasts
  developing, 62, 64
  male, at puberty, 64

California, weapons laws of, 129
California Attorney General's Office, 122
Cancer, cervical, 92
Car security, 126, 127
Castration, 69
Catheters, 179, 182
Centers for Disease Control (Atlanta), 105
Cervical cancer, 92
Cervical cap, 83, 91
Cervix in conception process, 75, 76
Chemical sprays (for self-defense), 129
Child sexual abuse, 157–58

of mentally retarded, 183
organizational help for, 197
Chilgren, R., 182
Coalition on Sexuality and Disability, 198
Coercion. *See* Rape/sexual coercion
Cole, T. M., 182
Coles, Robert, 121, 135, 159–60
Combination birth-control pills, 87
Communication, 6, 23–27, 35–52
  assessing comfort level of, 16–18
  basic rules of, 45–52
  establishing dialogue, 32–34
  establishing trust, 135–36
  evaluating messages communicated, 44–45
  with handicapped teenagers, 177–78, 180, 184–86
  about homosexuality, 114
  with homosexual teenagers, 169, 173–75
  listening, 45–47, 72, 136, 174
  of moral values, 39–41, 69, 72
  negative forms of, 45–48
  nonverbal, 13–14, 23–26, 44
  setting rules, 137–38
  with sexually active teenagers, 134–39
  sharing information, 48–50
  showing respect, 36–42
  using direct statements, 49–52
Comfort, level of
  assessing, 16–18
  See also Embarrassment
"Coming out," 170–71, 174
Conception
  handicapped's need for information on, 187, 188
  myths about, 76–77
  process of, 12, 29, 74–76
Condoms, 33, 34, 48–49, 76, 80–82, 139

how to use, 77–78, 81, 82, 84–85

providing teens with, 79, 80–81

and STDs, 76, 80–81, 100–101, 105, 106

types of, 81, 82, 100

Contraception, 11, 12, 19, 26, 33–34, 38, 48–49, 59, 76–94, 139

handicapped and, 183, 187–88

myths about, 76–77

"natural" methods of, 79–80

responsibility for, 78–79

teenagers' knowledge of, 76–79, 96, 149–50

teenagers' degree of use of, 79

See also specific methods

Contraceptive creams, 83, 89–90

Contraceptive foam, 76–78, 82, 83, 86, 100–101, 106, 139

Contraceptive jellies, 83, 89–90

Contraceptive sponge, 91–93

Contraceptive suppositories, 83, 86

Control, parents' desire for, 36–38, 70, 134, 137, 139, 140

Cosby, Bill, 21–22

Counseling, 32, 194

abortion and, 145

for children of single parents, 163

for handicapped, 180, 183, 185, 187, 189

for homosexual teenagers, 172, 174, 175

organizational resources and, 198–200

for parents of handicapped, 189

for parents of homosexuals, 167

for parents of rape victims, 156

pregnancy, 143–44

for sexual trauma, 152–55

for single parents, 164

Creams. *See* Contraceptive creams

Deaf teenagers, 185

Depression in handicapped, 178–79

Diaphragm (contraceptive), 76, 83, 89–91

Dieting, menstrual cycle and, 141

Dilation and curettage (D and C), 145

Dilation and evacuation (D and E), 145

Disabled. *See* Handicapped

Discrimination. *See* Prejudice

District of Columbia, 9

Divorce

sexual activity in children and, 159–60

teenage marriages and, 159

Doctors. *See* Physicians

Dolls, sex education for handicapped and, 184–85

Douches

as "contraceptive," 77

and spermicides, 83, 86, 87

Drug use

AIDS and, 96, 97, 99

forced sex and, 123

by handicapped, 179, 189

sexual activity and, 101

Eating disorders, 61

Egg (ovum), 75, 76

Ejaculation

and AIDS transmission, 97

in conception process, 75–77

nocturnal emissions, 63, 64

with onset of puberty, 62–64

Embarrassment

in children, 4, 11–12, 19–20, 29–30

about contraceptives, 79, 81–82

in handicapped, 179

in parents, 4, 6, 11–12, 15–18

and reporting of sexual coercion, 121, 151–52

Embarrassment *(cont'd)*
sexual assaults and, 155–56
about STDs, 104
Embryo, 76
Erection, prostheses and, 181
Exercise
during menstruation, 66
and onset of puberty, 61–62

Fallopian tubes, 75, 76
Family planning organizations,
79, 80, 139, 198
See also Planned Parenthood
Family Service Association of
America, 195, 198
Fears of parents, 7–12
Feminine hygiene sprays, 3, 34
Femininity
children of single parents and,
165–66
teens' concerns about, 111–12,
114
Fertility awareness
contraceptive methods, 79–80
Fertilization. *See* Conception
Fetus, 76
Florence Crittenton Association,
149, 197
Foam. *See* Contraceptive foam
Food and Drug Administration
(FDA), 87
Forced sex. *See* Rape/sexual coer-
cion
Foster care, 144, 148–49

Gang rape, 121, 123
Gay Community Services Center,
198–99
Gayellow Pages, 199
Gay Rights movement, 6–7
Gays
use of term, 115
See also Homosexuality
Gay Switchboard, 199

Gender differences
abortion and, 144
adoption and foster care and,
149
age and sexual experience and, 12
homosexuality and, 116–17
incidence of sex crimes and,
118–19
masturbation and, 68–69
onset of puberty and, 61–63
responsibility to partner and,
59
sex-educational reading matter
and, 29, 228–29
STD symptoms and, 107
talking to parents and, 20
vulnerability to AIDS and, 97
Gender identity, 14
adolescent fears about, 111–14
of children of single parents,
165–66
Genetic factors. *See* Heredity
Genitals, puberty and, 64
Ginott, Haim, 22
Girls vs. Boys. *See* Gender differences
Gonorrhea, 102, 104, 105
Gordon, Judith, 186
Gordon, Sol, 186
Grief
in children of separated parents,
163
in parents of homosexuals, 168
Growth spurt of puberty, 63–64
Guilt
about abortion, 144
in parents of homosexuals, 168–
69
in rape victims, 122, 127, 153
as weapon for parent, 69
Gynecomastia, 64

Hair growth at puberty, 64
Haiti, 96, 99

Handicapped, 176–89
  communicating with, 177–78, 180, 184–86
  hearing impairment, 184–85
  information sources for, 182, 224
  mental retardation, 182–84, 186
  motor disabilities, 180–82
  organizational help for, 198
  relationships formed by, 188–89
  secondary problems of, 178–80
  special information needs of, 187–88
  visual impairment, 184
Hass, Aaron, 20, 45–46, 68–69
Hearing-impaired teenagers, 185
Hemophiliacs, 96
Heredity
  and handicaps, 188
  and pubertal changes, 61, 64
Herpes, 102, 104
Herpes Resource Center, The, 200
Home security, 125–26
Homosexuality, 6–7, 110–17, 167–75
  AIDS and, 96, 97, 171, 173
  children of single parents and, 165
  "coming out," 170–71, 174
  communicating truth about, 114–17
  counseling and, 167, 172, 174, 175
  dealing with child's, 170–75
  definition of, 114, 169
  feelings of gay teenagers, 167–69, 171–72
  incidence of, 116–17
  organizational resources and, 198–99
  parent's feelings about child's, 110–11, 168–69, 172–75
  reading matter on, 167, 170, 171, 224–25
  teenage attitudes toward, 111–14, 168
Hormones, 9–10, 150
  birth control pills, 76, 87–89
  morning-after pills, 93
  See also Puberty
Human Immunodeficiency Virus (HIV), 96, 99, 100, 109

"I," use of, 49–51
Immune system, AIDS and, 96
Impotence in motor-handicapped, 180
Incest, 156–58
Independence, adolescent's need for, 36–38
Information sources, 139
  books as, 3, 29–32, 40, 62, 223–29
  on homosexuality, 167, 170, 171, 224–25
  for handicapped, 182, 224
  media as, 3, 9, 15, 31, 33–34, 57, 70, 72, 191
  parents as, 3–4, 8–15, 28, 32–34, 139, 191–92
  peers as, 15
  schools as, 8–9, 11
  subliminal, 13–15
  See also Professional help
Intrauterine devices (IUDs), 94
Irvine, University of California at, Rape Awareness and Prevention Program, 126–27
Isolation of handicapped, 179–80

Jellies. *See* Contraceptive jellies; Petroleum jelly
Johns Hopkins University, 8–9
Johnson, V., 192
J.T.C.P., 200

Kinsey, Alfred C., 116–17
Kissing, AIDS and, 96

Lady Chatterley's Lover (Lawrence), 180–81
Latex condoms, 81, 82, 100
Lawrence, D. H., 180–81
Legal rights, 225
Lesbians
    use of term, 114–15
    See also Homosexuality
Library books, 31
Listening, 45–47, 72, 136, 174
Lovett, Raymond E., 9–10
Lubricants, oil-based, 81

Magazines, 3, 9, 33
Marital status of parents, children's attitudes and, 159–60
Marriage
    handicapped teenagers and 188–89
    teenage pregnancies and, 148
    See also Divorce
Martial arts, 128
Maryland, 9
Masculinity
    children of single parents and, 165–66
    teenagers' concern about, 111–14
Masters, W. H., 192
Masturbation, 41, 64, 68–70, 113, 138
    mental retardation and, 183
Maturity of child
    readiness for information and, 18–21
    readiness for sexual experience and, 58
    See also Puberty
Media, 3, 9, 15, 31, 33–34, 57, 70, 72, 191
Medications, handicapped and, 179, 189

Menarche, 18, 62, 63, 65–66
Menstrual sponges, 66
Menstruation
    birth control pills and, 89
    irregularity of, in teenagers, 80, 141
    onset of, 18, 62, 63, 65–66
    physiology of, 66
    reading matter on, 229
Mentally retarded teenagers, 182–84, 186
Minipill, 87, 88
Miracle of Life, The (videotape), 74
Molestation, sexual, 157–58
    See also Child sexual abuse; Rape/sexual coercion
Mooney, T., 182
Moral values, 98
    communication of, 39–41, 69, 72
    masturbation and, 69, 72
    responsibility and, 58–59
    sex education and, 6–7, 38
    single parents and, 164–65
    of teenagers, respect for, 36, 38–41
Morning-after pills, 93
Motor-handicapped teenagers, 180–82
Movies, 3, 15, 33, 57, 70

National Abortion Federation Hotline, 197
National Abortion Rights League, 197
National AIDS Hotline, 197
National Right to Life Committee, 197
"Natural" birth control, 79–80
Netherlands, 9
New Jersey, 9
Newspapers, 3, 31, 33, 72, 114
Nocturnal emissions ("wet dreams"), 63, 64
Nonoxynol-9, 82, 83, 100, 106

Opinions. *See* Moral values
Oral contraceptives. *See* Birth control pills
Oral sex, 97, 100, 106
Organizations, listed, 196–200
Orgasm
  conception and, 77
  masturbation and, 68
Ovaries, 76
Ovum (egg), 75, 76

Paraplegics, 180–82
Parental relationship, 14
Parent-child interaction
  books on, 226
  and child's self-esteem, 56
  conflicts of adolescence and, 21–23, 25–28, 35–42
  early, 13–15, 67–68
  giving permission, 56–58, 79
  and homosexual teenagers, 169, 170, 173–75
  and menarche, 65
  parent's desire for control, 36–38, 70, 134, 137, 139, 140
  after sexual assault, 153–56
  in single-parent families, 161, 163
  See also Communication; Embarrassment
Parenthood, unplanned pregnancy and, 146–48
Parents and Friends of Lesbians and Gays (Parents FLAG), 199
Parents United, 197
Parents Without Partners, 162, 200
Passive resistance, 127–28
Pawlowski, Wayne V., 168
Peers, 15, 58, 71, 123
Pelvic inflammatory disease, 83, 94
Penis
  fears about size of, 112

masturbation and, 68, 69
  at puberty, 64
Periods. *See* Menstruation
Permission, giving, 56–58, 79
Personal hygiene of handicapped, 179
Petroleum jelly
  and condoms, 81
  and diaphragm, 90–91
Petting, 70
  motor handicaps and, 181
  STDs and, 104
Phone books, 152–53, 195–96
Physicians, 80, 139, 180, 194
  rape and, 152, 155
Pill, the. *See* Birth control pills
Pimples, 64–65
  masturbation and, 69
Planned Parenthood Federation of America, 195, 198
  abortion referrals from, 146
  adoption referrals from, 149
  natural birth control and, 80
  parenting skills and, 147
  pregnancy counseling from, 143
  pregnancy tests from, 141
Police, rape and, 129, 152, 153, 155
Pregnancy, 3–4, 33, 38, 49, 50, 59, 70, 140–50
  books on, 226
  choosing abortion, 144–46
  choosing adoption or foster care, 148–49
  choosing parenthood, 144–48
  confirming, 141–42
  handicapped teenagers and, 187, 188
  incidence of, among teenagers, 4, 140
  marriage in, 148
  sex education and, 5–6, 8–9, 149
  teenage parents' reactions to, 137–38, 141

Pregnancy (*cont'd*)
traumatic aspects of, 140–41
See also Abortion; Contraception
Prejudice
against handicapped, 180
against homosexuals, 170–73
Privacy
for discussing sex, 48
respecting adolescent's need for, 36, 41–42
Professional help, 193–200
getting referrals, 193–95
organizations listed by area of concern, 196–200
using phone book, 195–96
See also Counseling; Psychologists; Psychotherapists
Prostheses, 181
Prostitutes, AIDS and, 99
Psychologists/psychiatrists, 152, 194
and handicapped, 189
Psychotherapy
for handicapped, 181, 187
homosexuality and, 172
See also Counseling
Puberty, 18, 61–66
age of onset of, 18–19, 61, 66
masturbation and, 68
menarche, 18, 62, 63, 65–66
physical changes of, 62–64

Quadriplegics, 181–82

Radio, 9
Raising a Child Conservatively in a Sexually Permissive World (Gordon and Gordon), 186
Rape/sexual coercion, 59, 70–72, 118–29, 151–58
by acquaintances, 71, 121–23
books on, 226–27
dealing with assaults, 127–29

dealing with trauma of, 151–56
gender differences and, 118–19
incestuous, 156–58
incidence of, 121, 151,
rape defense programs, 129
reducing risk of, 122–24
security precautions against, 124–27
Rape crisis centers, 152–55
Rebellion, adolescent, 37–38, 48, 138
Rectum, AIDS transmission via, 100
Religion, 33, 69, 80, 144, 155, 227
See also Moral values
Repetitiveness, fear of, 11
Respect, need for, 36–42
Responsibility
for contraception, 78–79
moral values and, 58–59
of parenthood, 146–47
sexual, for self-protection, 119–22
of teenage marriage, 148
"Rhythm method," 79–80
Rules, setting, 137–38

Safer sex, 12, 95, 96, 98–101
Safety, 49
contracting with teenagers about, 38
response to sexual assault, 127–29
security precautions, 124–27
from sexual exploitation, 119–20, 122–29
Saliva, AIDS and, 96, 97
Sanitary napkins, 34, 66
Schools, sex education in, 8–9, 11
Scrotum, 64
Security. *See* Safety
Self-esteem, Pill's side effects and, 89

Semen. *See* Sperm

Separation. *See* Divorce; Single parents

Sex Information and Education Council of the United States, 148, 199–200

Sex Information Hot Line, 199

"Sex lectures," 7–8, 32–33

Sex-related differences. *See* Gender differences

Sex therapy, 16, 199–200
for handicapped, 181

Sexual abuse. *See* Child sexual abuse; Rape/sexual coercion

Sexual aids, 181

Sexual Assault Prevention Handbook (California Attorney General's Office), 122

Sexual coercion. *See* Rape/sexual coercion

Sexual intercourse
and AIDS, 97, 98, 100
and conception, 74–77
first, age of, 9, 12
marital status of parents and, 159–60
motor handicaps and, 181–82
and STDs, 105–6
talking about, 70

Sexually transmitted diseases (STDs), 5–6, 11, 12, 49, 59, 70, 102–9, 139
books on, 228
contraceptives and, 76, 81–83, 92, 96, 98, 100–101, 105, 106
incidence of, among young people, 4–5, 105
informing partners about, 104, 108–9
organizational help and, 200
preventive measures against, 105–7
symptoms of, 107–8
transmission of, 103–5

treatment of, 108–9
See also AIDS

Sexual Options for Paraplegics and Quadriplegics (Mooney, Cole, and Chilgren), 182

Shame. *See* Embarrassment; Guilt

Single parents, 159–66
attitudes of children of, 159–60
and children's feeling of loss, 163
gender identity of children of, 165–66
organizational help for, 200
sexual life of, and children, 161, 163–65
support groups for, 162
time spent with children by, 161–62

Skin problems, 64–65

Social skills of handicapped, 180

Sperm (semen)
and AIDS transmission, 97
in conception, 74–76
survival of, in female's body, 80
See also Ejaculation

Spermicides. *See* Vaginal spermicides

Sterilization, 94
handicapped and, 183, 187

Stokes, Geoffrey, 121, 135, 159–60

Stomas, 182

Suicide, 138

Support groups for single parents, 162

Suppositories, contraceptive, 83, 86

Sweden, 9

Syphilis, 102, 104, 105

Talc, 90–91

Tampons, 34, 66

Tears, AIDS transmission and, 97

Telephone books, 152–53, 195–96

Television, 3, 9, 15, 33, 57, 72, 186
  and attitudes toward rape, 70
Testes (testicles), 64
Therapy. *See* Psychotherapy; Sex
  therapy
Touching, 14, 67–68
Toxic Shock Syndrome, 66, 92
Transsexuality, 200
Trust, establishing, 135–36
Tubal ligation, 94

Unattractiveness, handicapped
  teenager's feelings of, 179
Uterus
  in conception, 75, 76
  IUDs and, 94

Vacuum-aspiration abortions, 145
Vagina in conception process, 75
Vaginal intercourse
  AIDS and, 97, 98, 100
  See also Sexual intercourse
Vaginal products, non-contracep-
  tive, 87
Vaginal contraceptive film, 87
Vaginal spermicides, 76–78, 82–
  87, 100, 105, 106
  in contraceptive sponge, 92
  with diaphragm or cervical cap,
  83, 89–91
Values. *See* Moral values
Vasectomy, 94
Vaseline
  and condoms, 81

and diaphragm, 90–91
VD National Hotline, 200
Vehicle security, 126, 127
Venereal disease (VD). *See* Sex-
  ually transmitted diseases
  (STDs)
Verbal ability of handicapped, 179
Vibrators, 181
Visually impaired teenagers, 184–
  85
Voice, "cracking" of, 63

Way of Love, A Way of Life, A
  (Hanckel and Cunningham,
  171
Weight
  birth control pills and, 89
  eating disorders and, 61
Weapons for self-defense, 129
"Wet dreams" (nocturnal emissions), 63, 64
Women's liberation movement,
  6–7

Yellow pages, 195–96
YMCA, 129
Young Man's Guide to Sex, A
  (Gale), 62, 77, 103
Young Woman's Guide to Sex, A
  (Voss and Gale), 30–31, 62,
  77, 103, 122
YWCA, 129

Zero Population Growth, 198